The Ultimate Cartoon Book of Book Cartoons
by the World's Greatest Cartoonists

THE
ULTIMATE
CARTOON BOOK
OF
BOOK
CARTOONS

by the
World's Greatest Cartoonists

Bob Eckstein, editor

PRINCETON ARCHITECTURAL PRESS · NEW YORK

Introduction

The world's greatest cartoonists drawing about books and bookstores—this, I thought to myself, is a book that needs no introduction.

Not everyone agreed (or at least, nobody at Princeton Architectural Press). While I assumed nobody even *reads* the introduction, I am being proven wrong right now because here you are. And that's good because there is an important backstory I'd like to share.

One of the all-time great cartoon tropes is the "Meet the Author" cartoon (see pages 40, 50, 63, 118, 122, 127, 128, and 135). I think this is because the release of tension is a key component in making a joke work, and there is nothing more tense than a book event. As any bookstore owner will tell you, a lot can go wrong at a book event. I was an author before I became a cartoonist and had many disasters. I once had a book event during a blizzard where only two braved the weather, and I'm counting some

guy who was there only to crash on the couch. Even Hemingway, gutsy Ernest Hemingway, was known to drag a friend along to read first—plus, he would stash whiskey under the table to settle his nerves.

But when they go right, they go right. When readers engage with the author it can form a special relationship. Like the ones we have with books. Books are often better than the movie. They can make you laugh, cry, or think in ways you hadn't imagined. The very first book I read shaped my life and who I am today. For those unfamiliar with *Go, Dog. Go!*, it involves a group of highly mobile canines driving to some party in a big tree on the horizon. Our protagonists are three dogs (pink, yellow, and blue) wearing racing goggles. Even then—I was a very self-aware five-year-old—I realized author P. D. Eastman was using this day trip as a metaphor for the journey of life, teaching us to remember where we come from and where we are going; that life isn't one big party (or maybe it is); the lessons of rejection (Male dog, "Do you like my hat?" Female dog, "No I do not."); and the importance of a good work ethic (to go, go, go with dogged tenacity), lessons that stick with me today. Because books have that ability.

The book in your hands is a direct result of my last book, *Footnotes from the World's Greatest Bookstores.* In writing about independent bookstores, I met with dozens of bookstore owners and heard hundreds of bookstore stories (including every falling-in-love-in-a-bookstore story and every cute-bookstore-cat story). I feel indebted to this hardworking group for their support, and thought, What better love letter to them—and to all book lovers—than a collection of book cartoons that would make them laugh and also show them how much they are appreciated? Bookstores are the cultural hubs of our Main Streets, and not enough can be said for what they do for our communities, our youth, our writers, and our growth.

This book was also a chance to do a project with another group of professionals I deeply respect and admire: cartoonists. This book includes my favorite cartoonists (and many cartoons that have never been published before), and I am so excited to share their work with you. They, too, are trying to keep alive a challenged, yet vibrant, institution that is also trying to find its proper place on that ever-growing, impersonal information highway. I think it's appropriate to make the connection between the worlds of cartoons and physical bookstores and books, as any of them would be greatly missed if they ever disappeared. Let's make sure physical books never get completely replaced by bytes, bookstores by drones, or cartoonists by robots.

I hope you enjoy this book. Long live books, bookstores, and cartoons! To whoever invented these wonderful things, my heartfelt thanks.

—*Bob Eckstein*

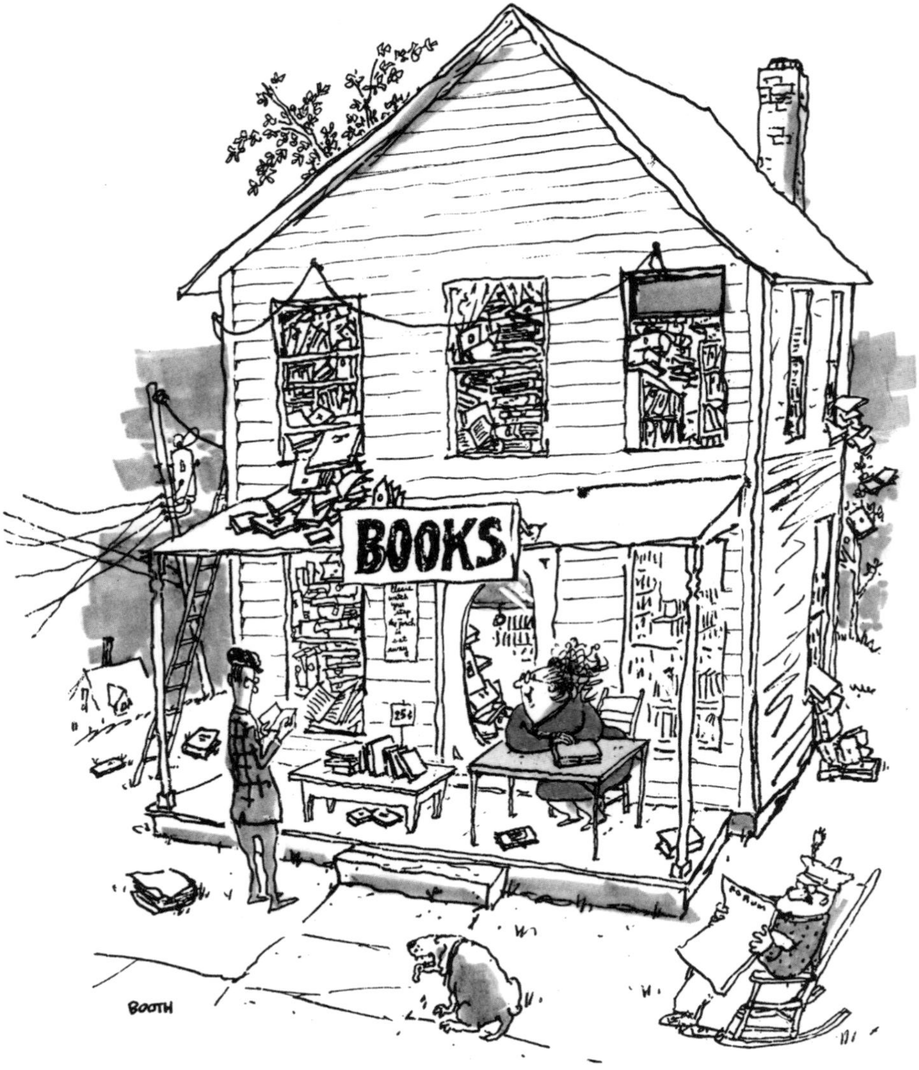
BOOKS
25¢
BOOTH

"There's plenty more books inside."

"I can't help thinking there's a book in this."

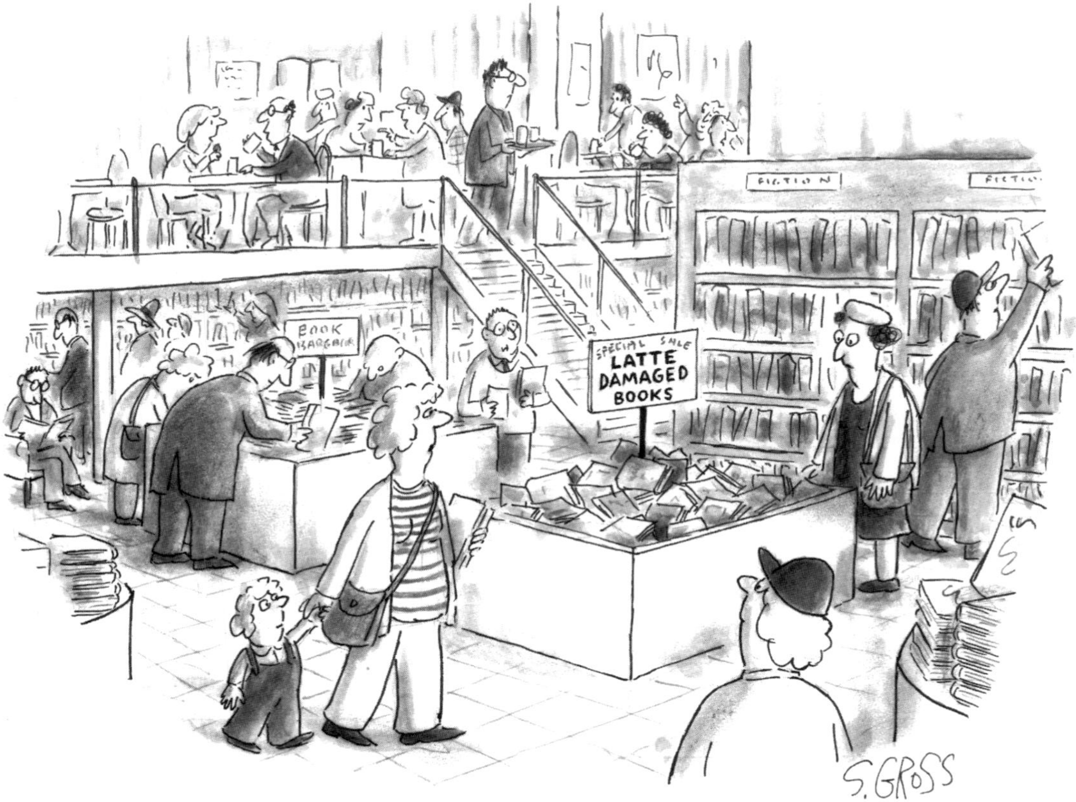
BOOK BARGAINS
SPECIAL SALE
LATTE DAMAGED BOOKS
FICTION
S. GROSS

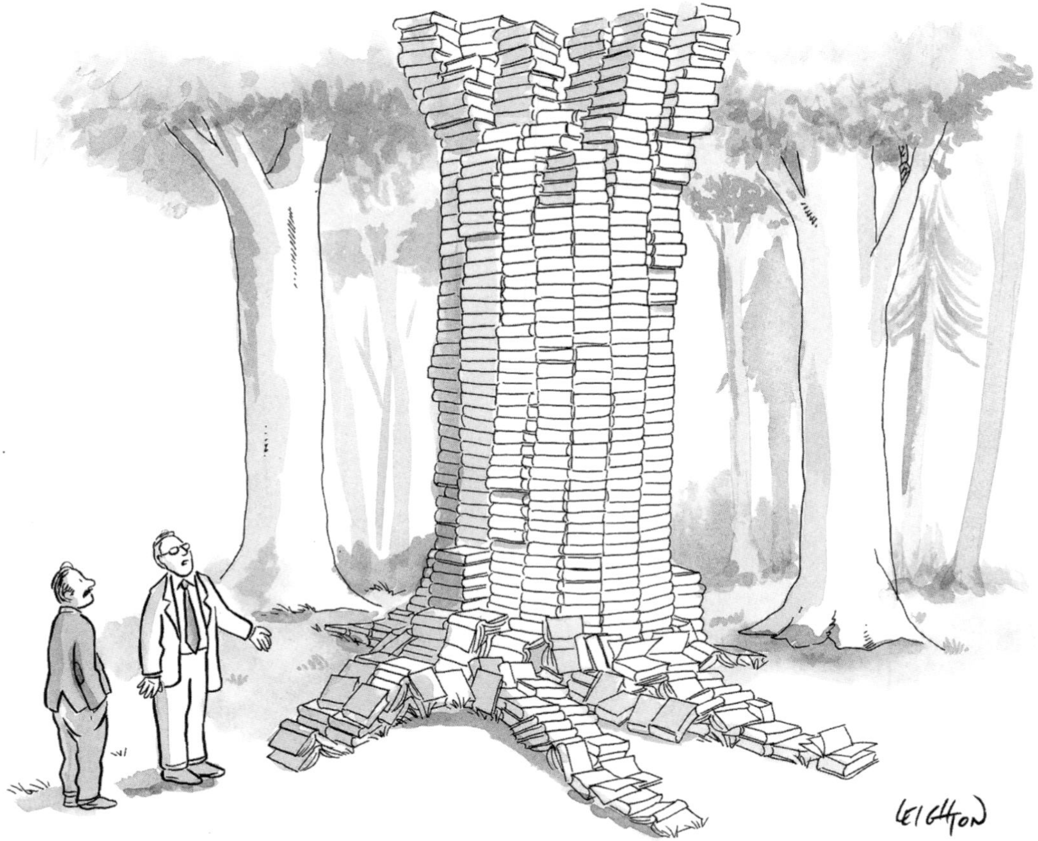
LEIGHTON

"We used your unsold copies to build a tree, but it's not the same."

"I enjoyed it and it definitely made me want to read more by this author."

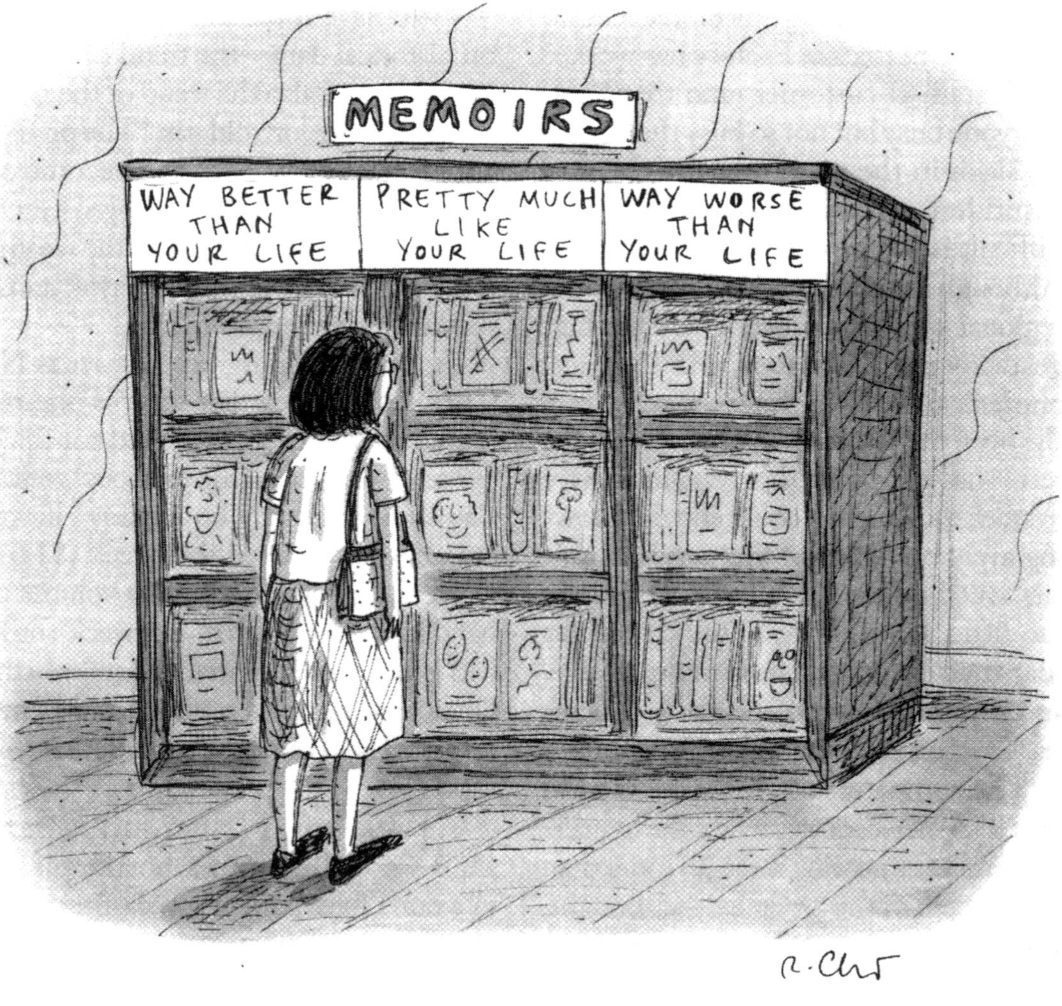
MEMOIRS
WAY BETTER THAN YOUR LIFE
PRETTY MUCH LIKE YOUR LIFE
WAY WORSE THAN YOUR LIFE

"Yes, but what I really want to do is write children's books."

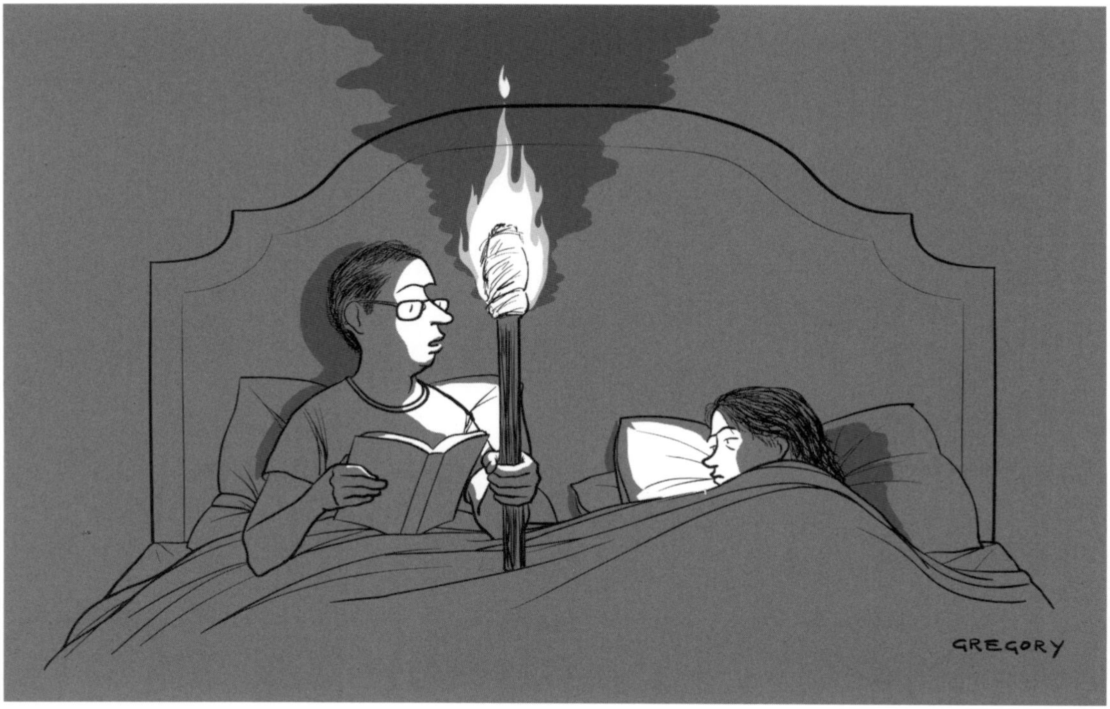
GREGORY

"Is the light bothering you?"

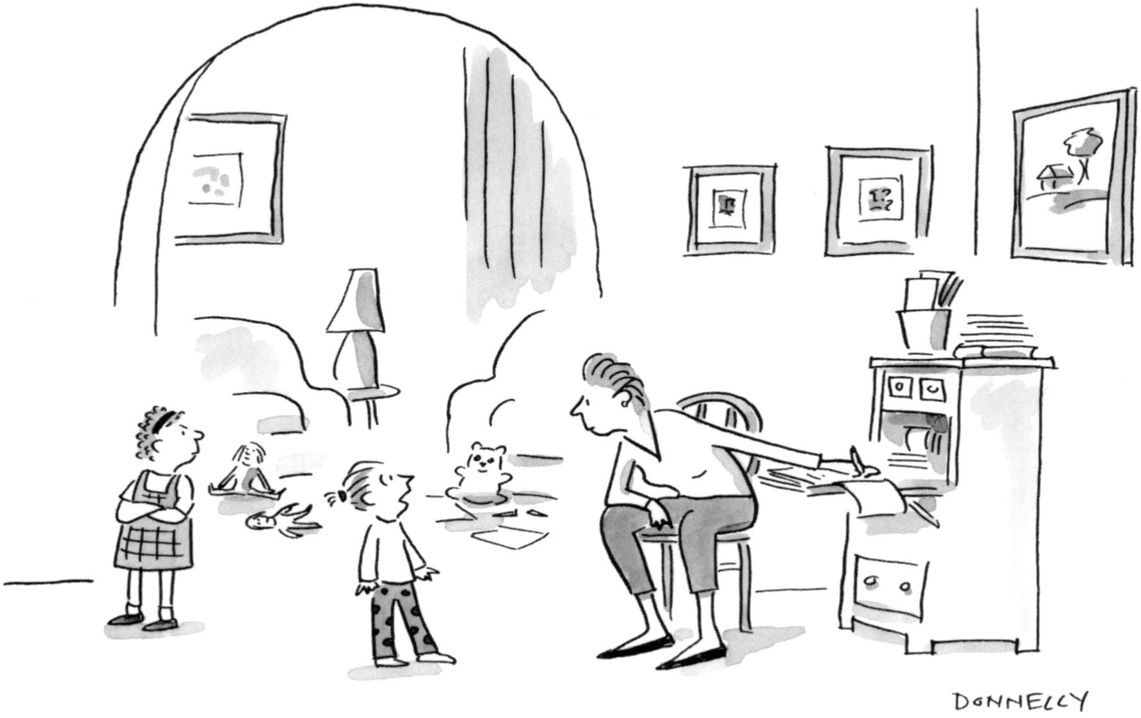
DONNELLY

“Mommy, Becky says she’s not going to put me in her memoirs!”

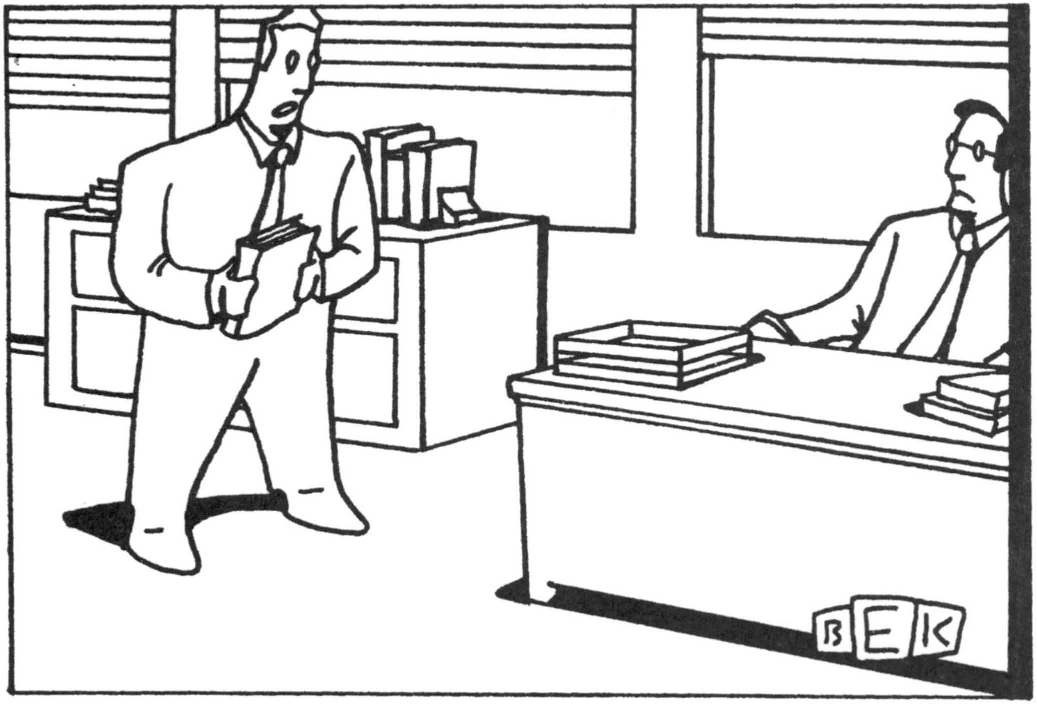
BEK

"Sometimes you just option it because your gut tells you
this is a book that has to be butchered."

"How's your book coming?"

"I tried self-publishing, but it just led to self-rejection."

"Now you're just being a jerk!"

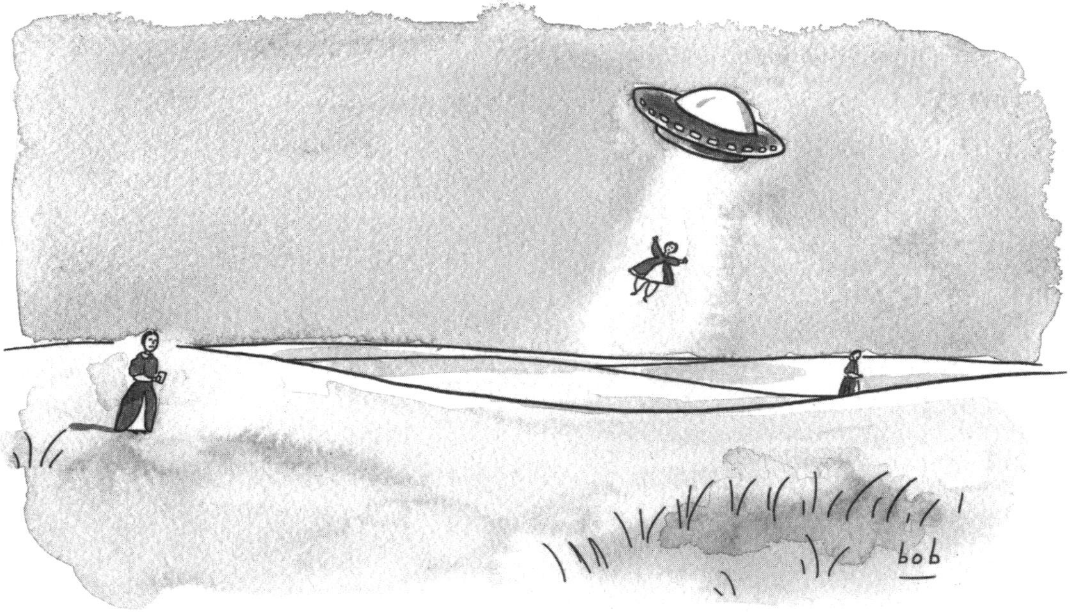
bob

If the Brontë Sisters Wrote Science Fiction

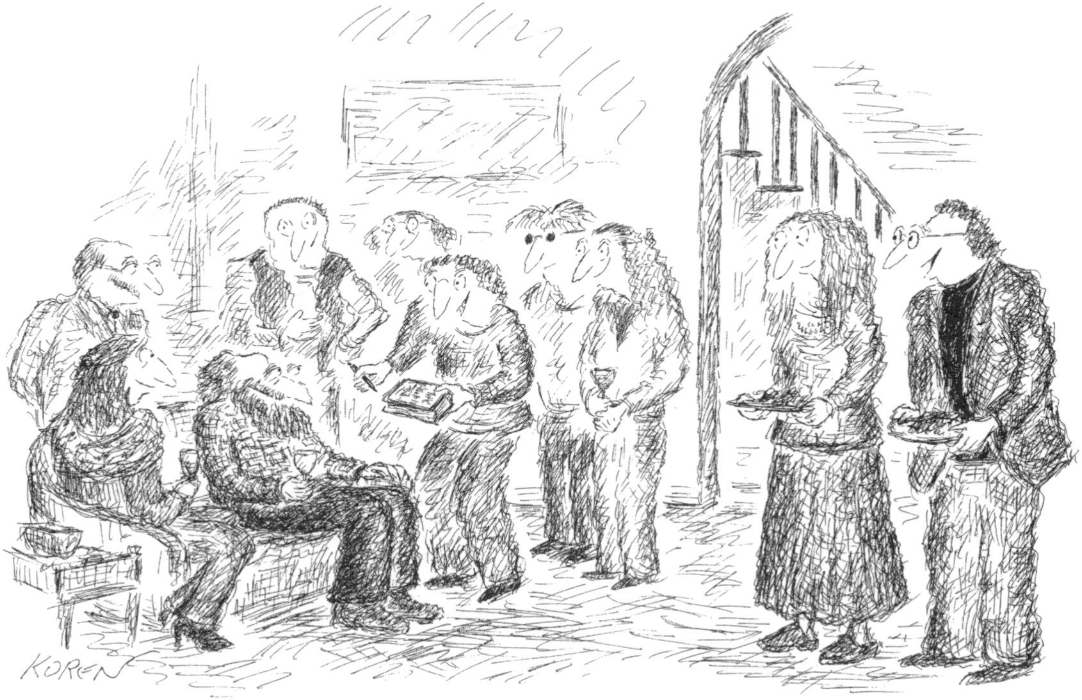
KOREN

"Stan is one of our great, widely unread literary treasures."

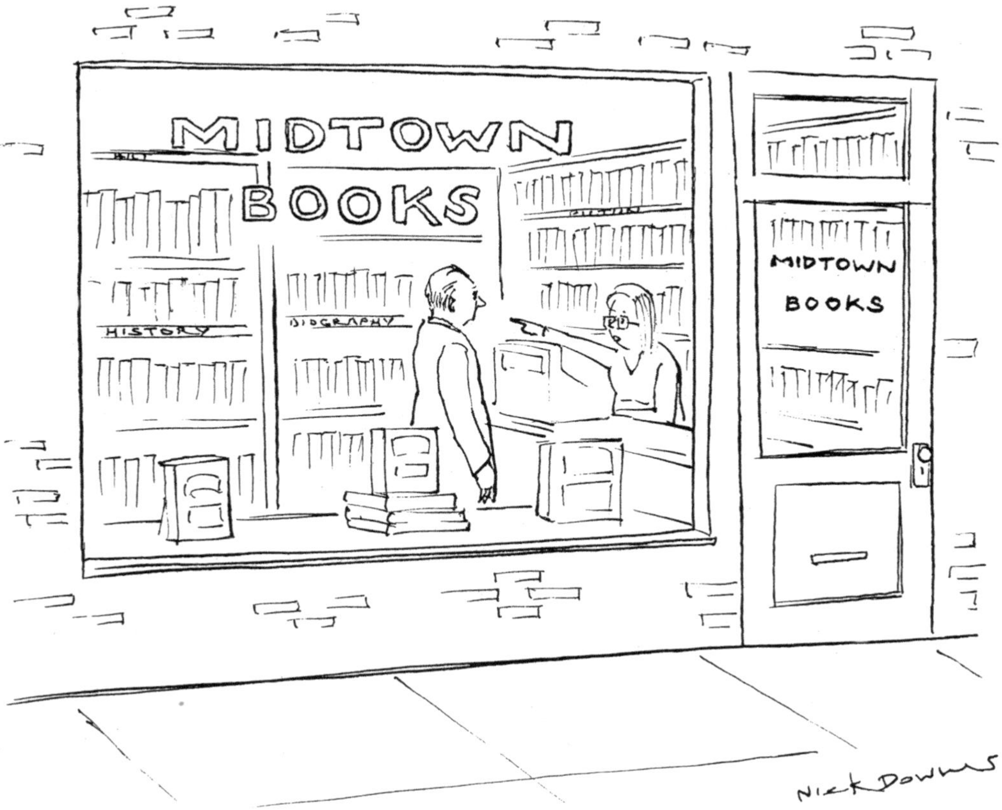
MIDTOWN
BOOKS
HISTORY
BIOGRAPHY
MIDTOWN
BOOKS

"Crossword puzzles? You might look under 'Colossal Wastes of Time.'"

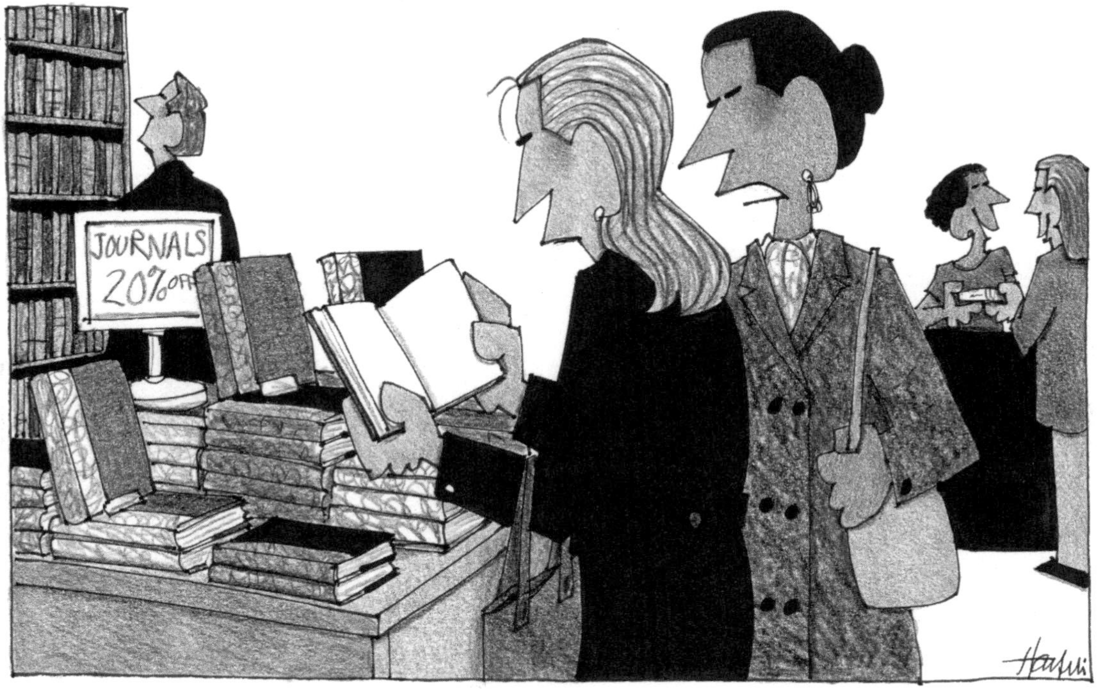
JOURNALS
20%

"I see no point in putting my thoughts on any paper that isn't archival quality."

"And then we are led to believe that they lived happily ever after."

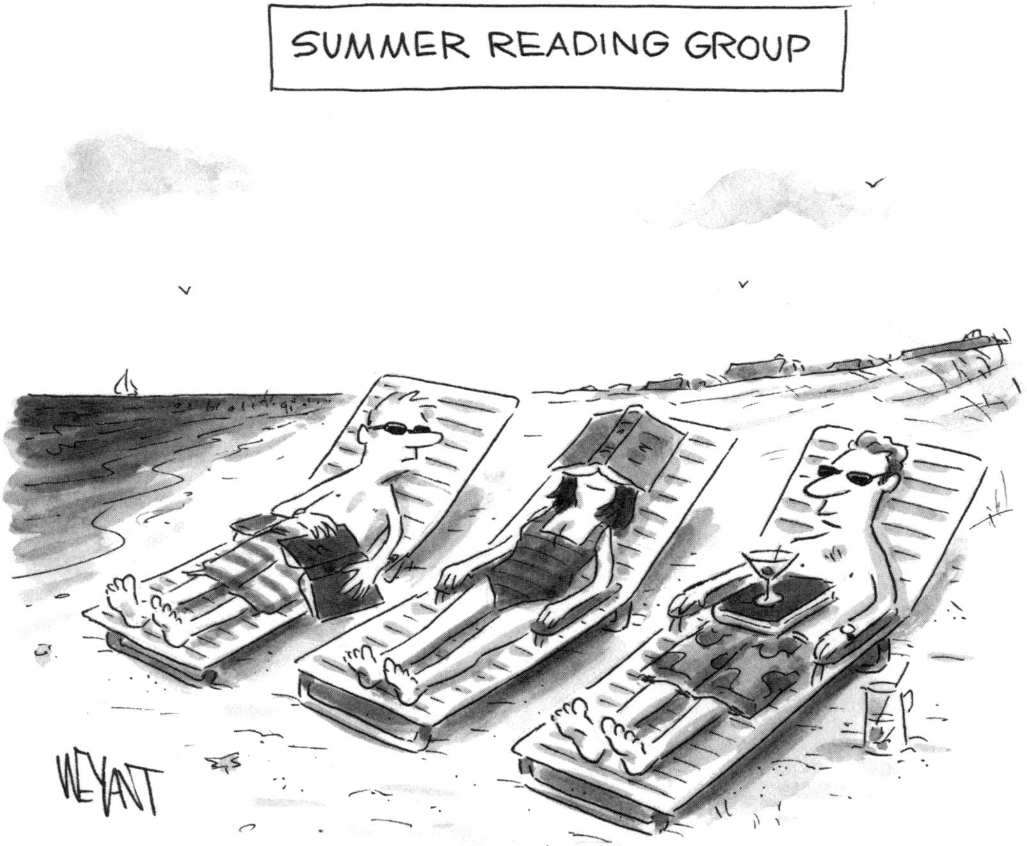
SUMMER READING GROUP
WEYANT

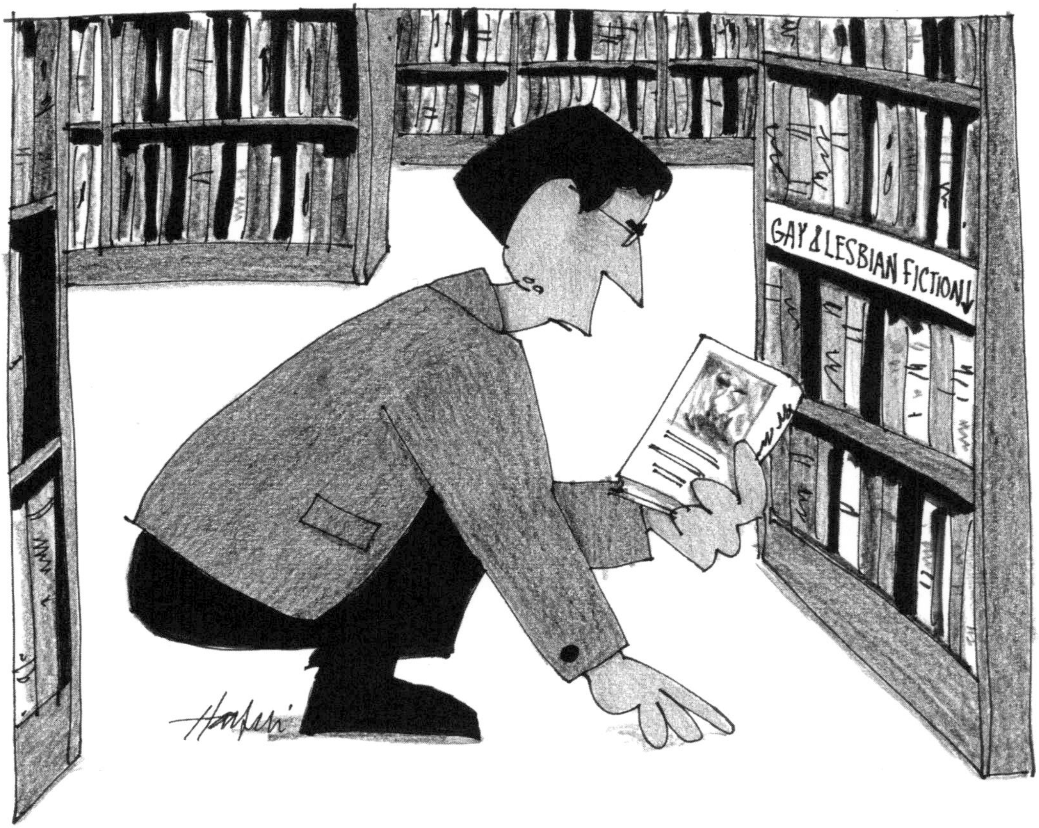
GAY & LESBIAN FICTION

"A literary masterpiece…Destined for obscurity…"

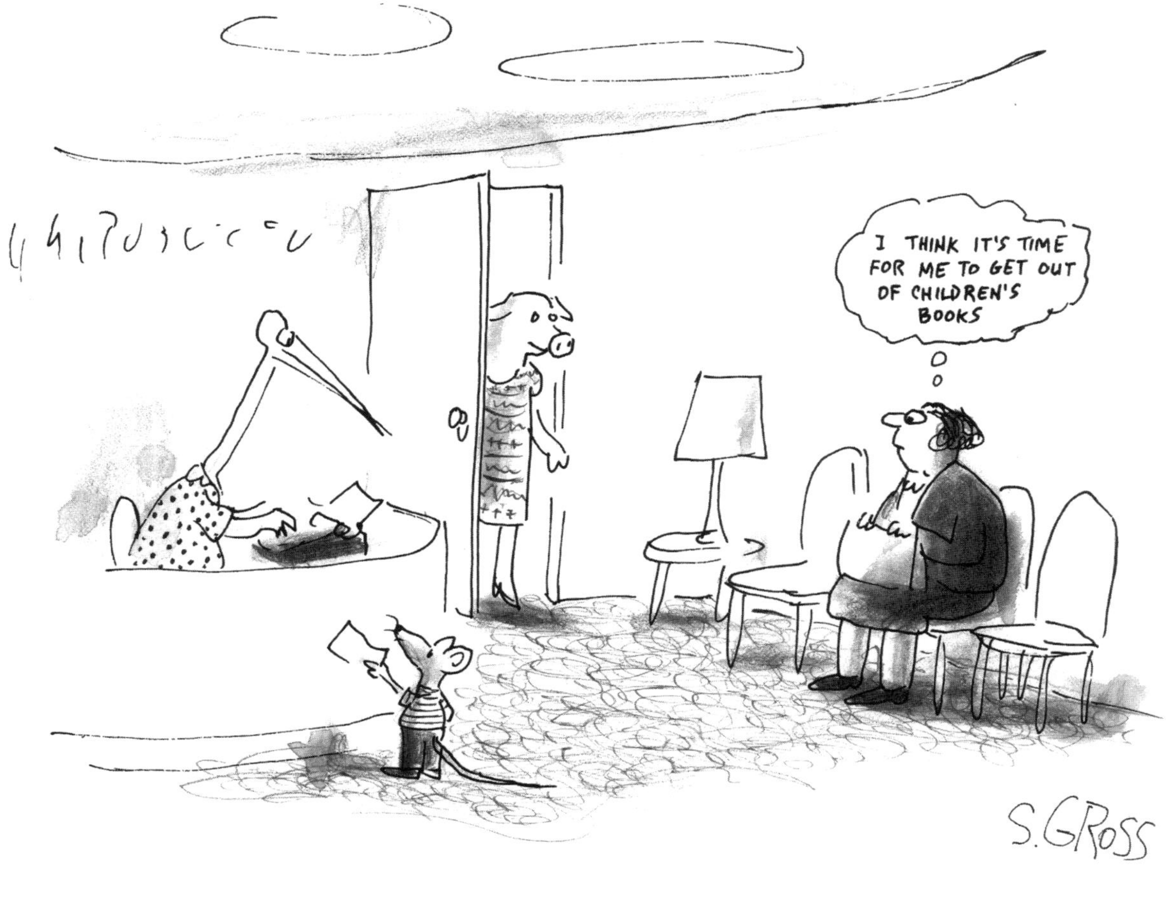
I THINK IT'S TIME FOR ME TO GET OUT OF CHILDREN'S BOOKS
S. GROSS

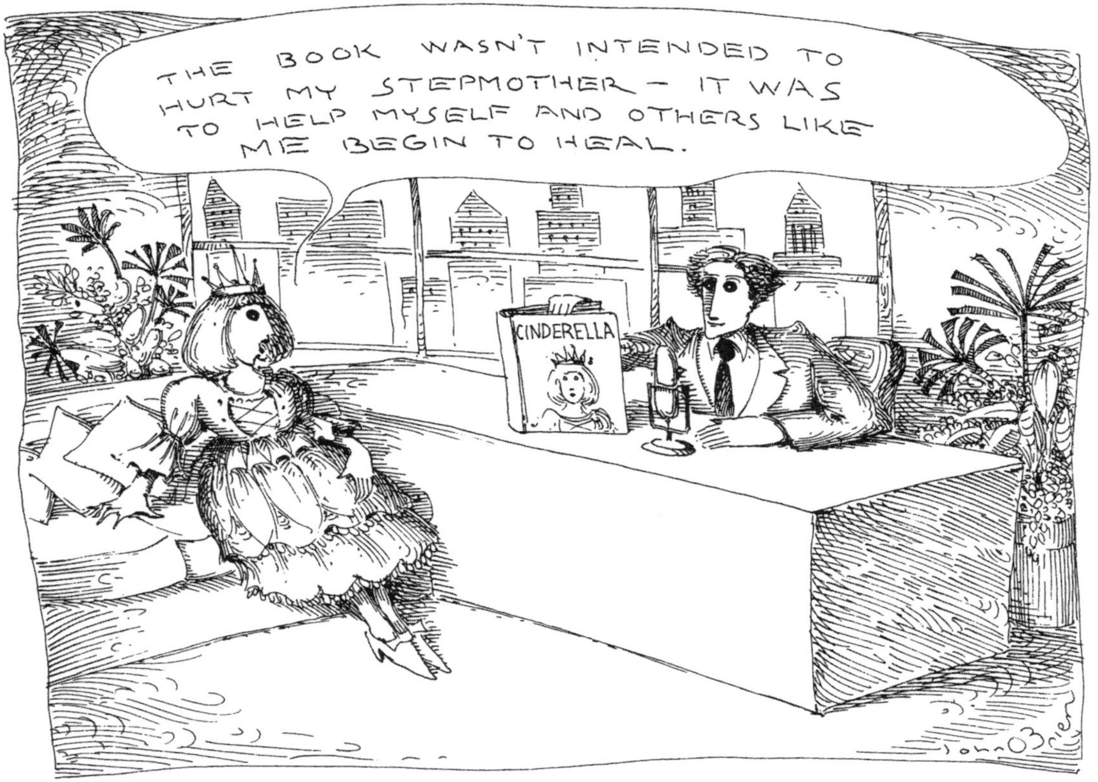
THE BOOK WASN'T INTENDED TO HURT MY STEPMOTHER – IT WAS TO HELP MYSELF AND OTHERS LIKE ME BEGIN TO HEAL.
CINDERELLA
John O'Brien

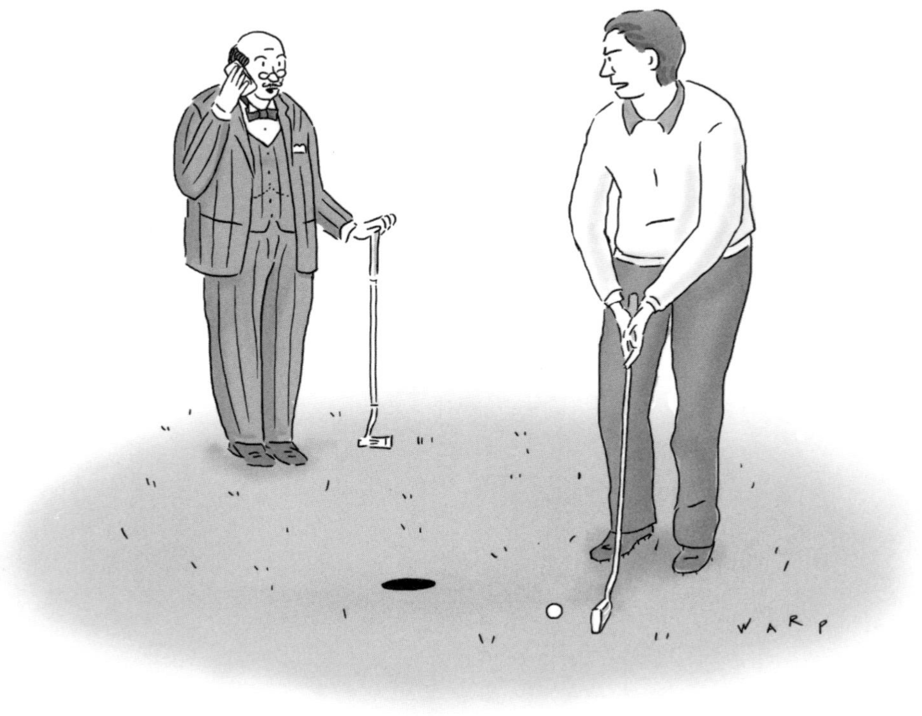
WARP

"Listen, Poirot, if you don't shut up there's going to be another murder on the links."

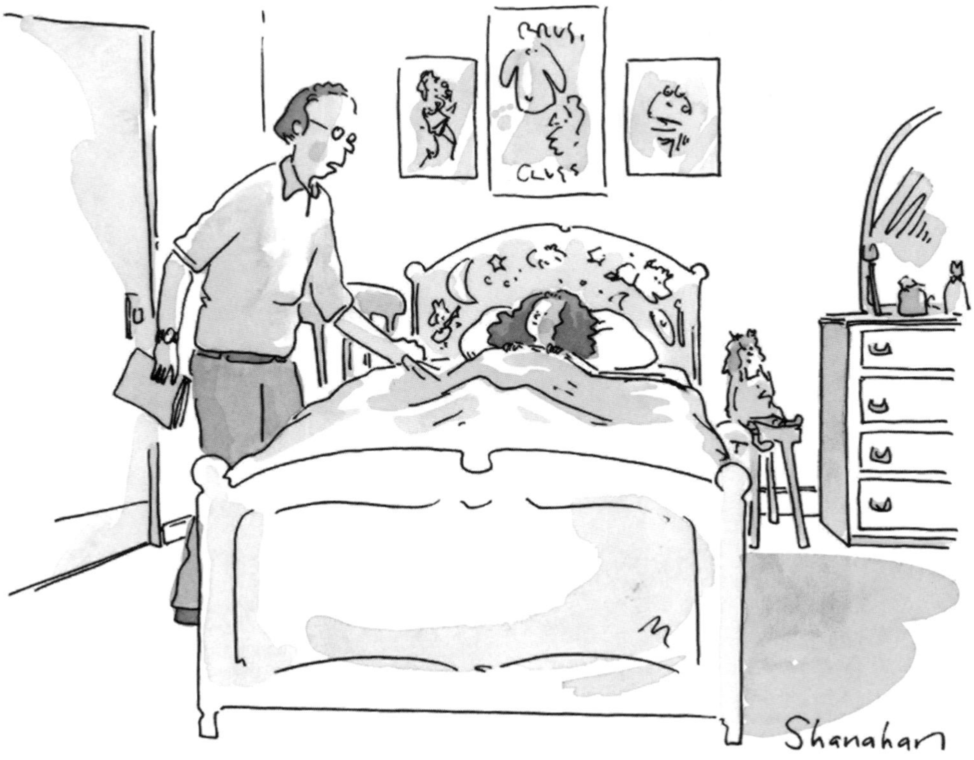
Shanahan

"Now close your eyes and go to sleep or Daddy will read you more of his novel."

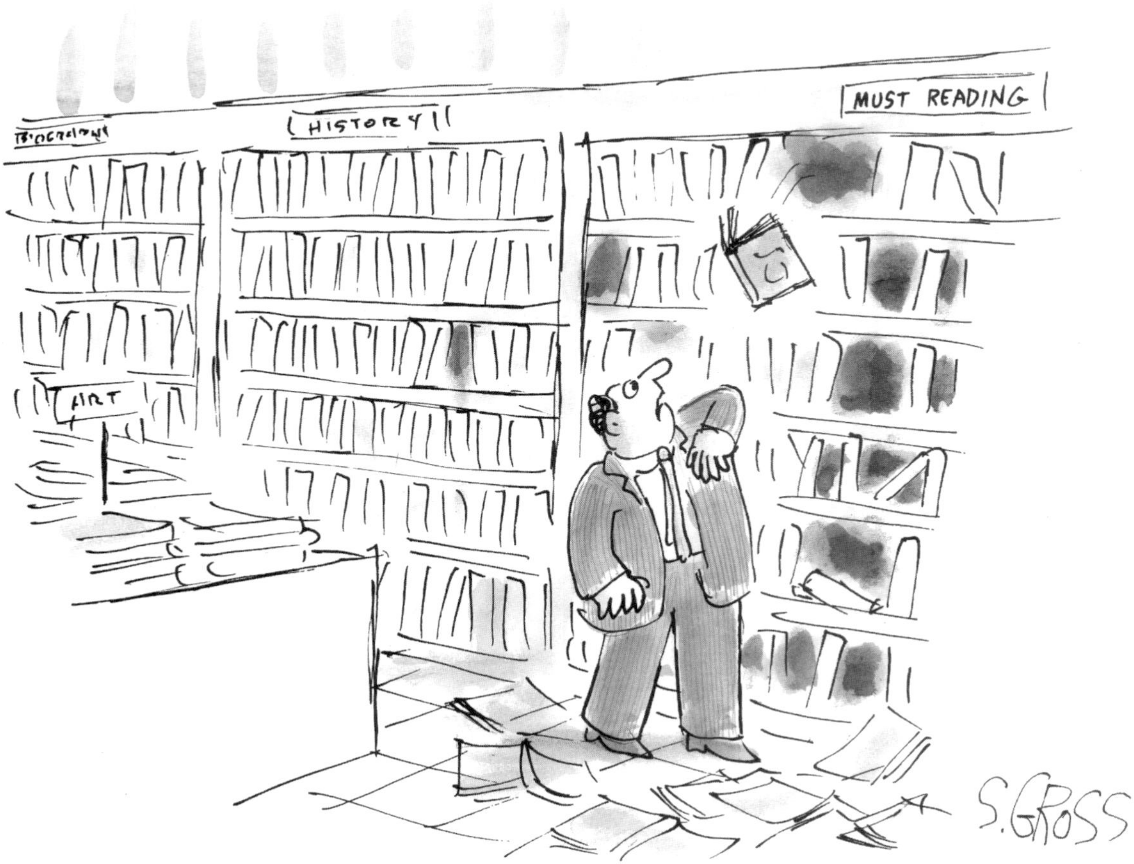
MUST READING
HISTORY
ART
S. GROSS

"The series is over, but there's an upside—we'll never have to read again."

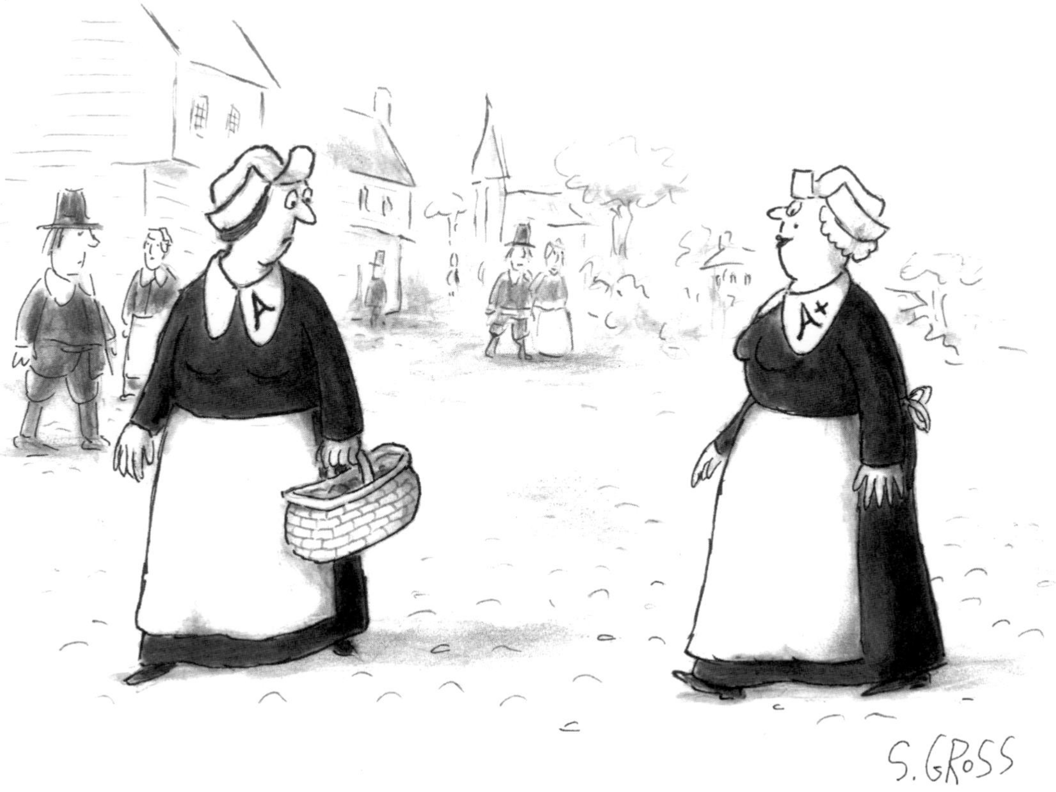
A
A+
S. GROSS

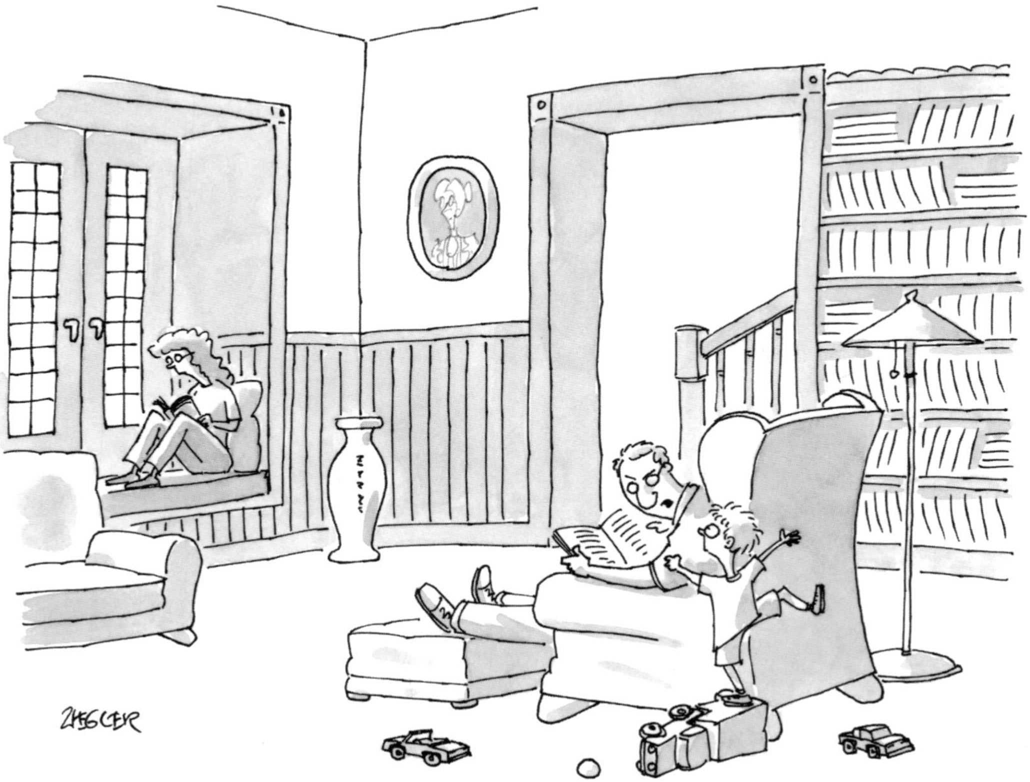
ZIEGLER

“Go bother your mother. She’s only reading chick lit.”

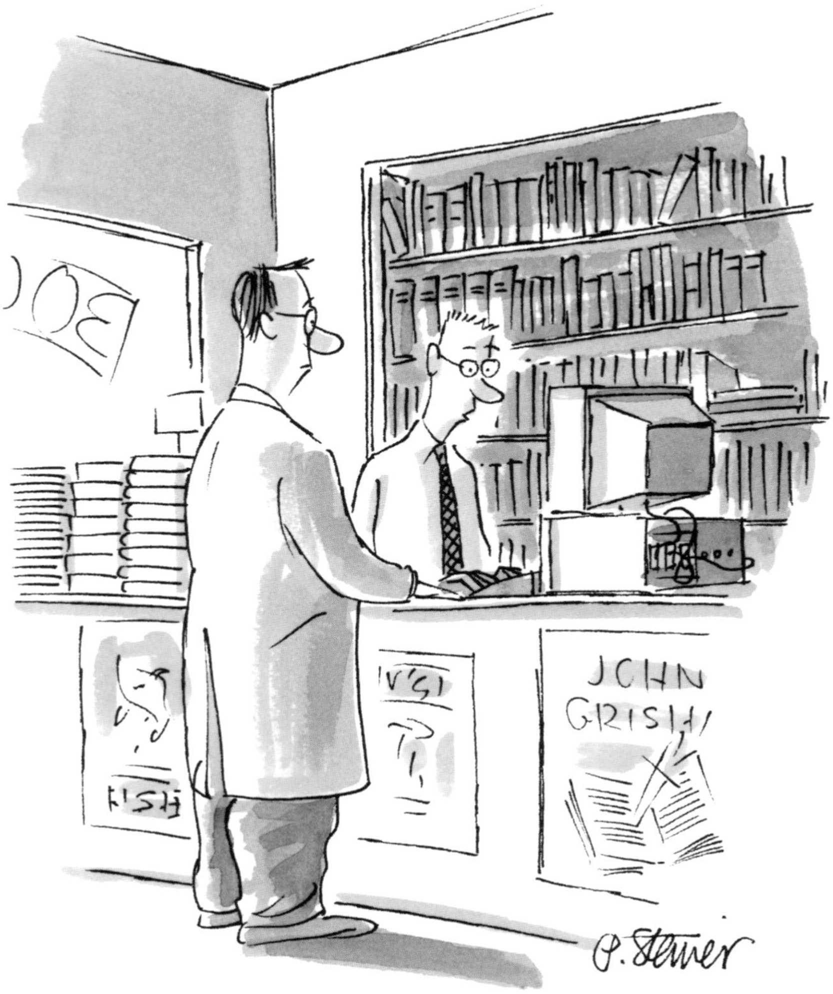
JOHN
GRISH

"The Bible... that would be under self-help."

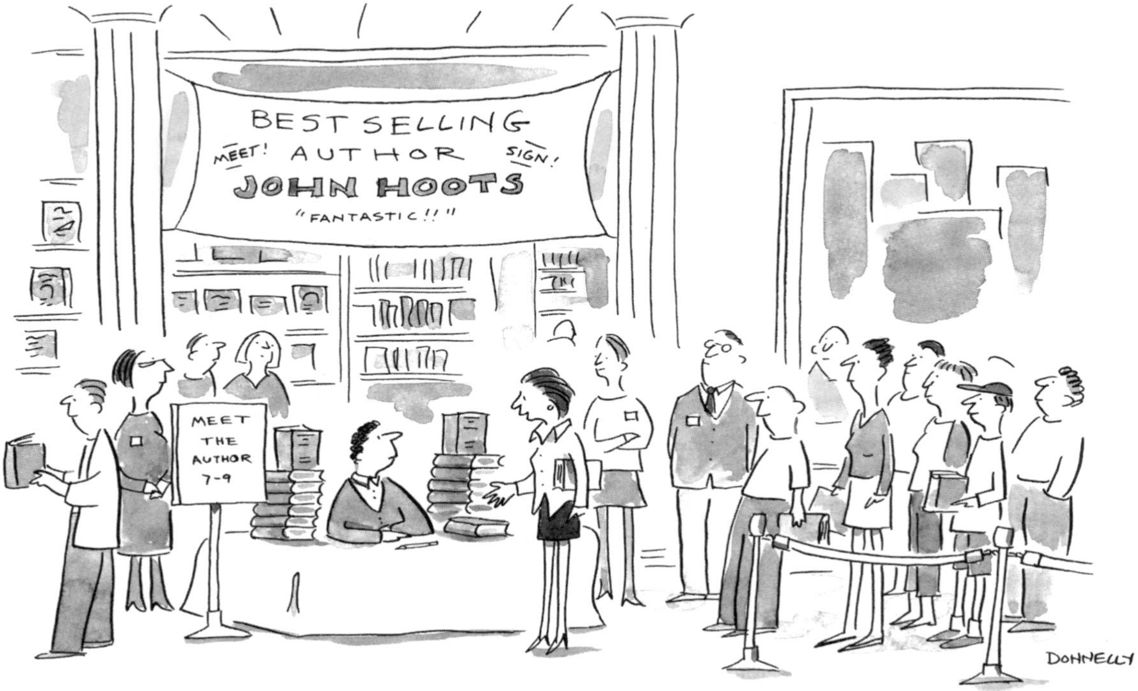
BEST SELLING
MEET! AUTHOR SIGN!
JOHN HOOTS
"FANTASTIC!!"
MEET THE AUTHOR 7-9
DONNELLY

"I really, really enjoyed your hype."

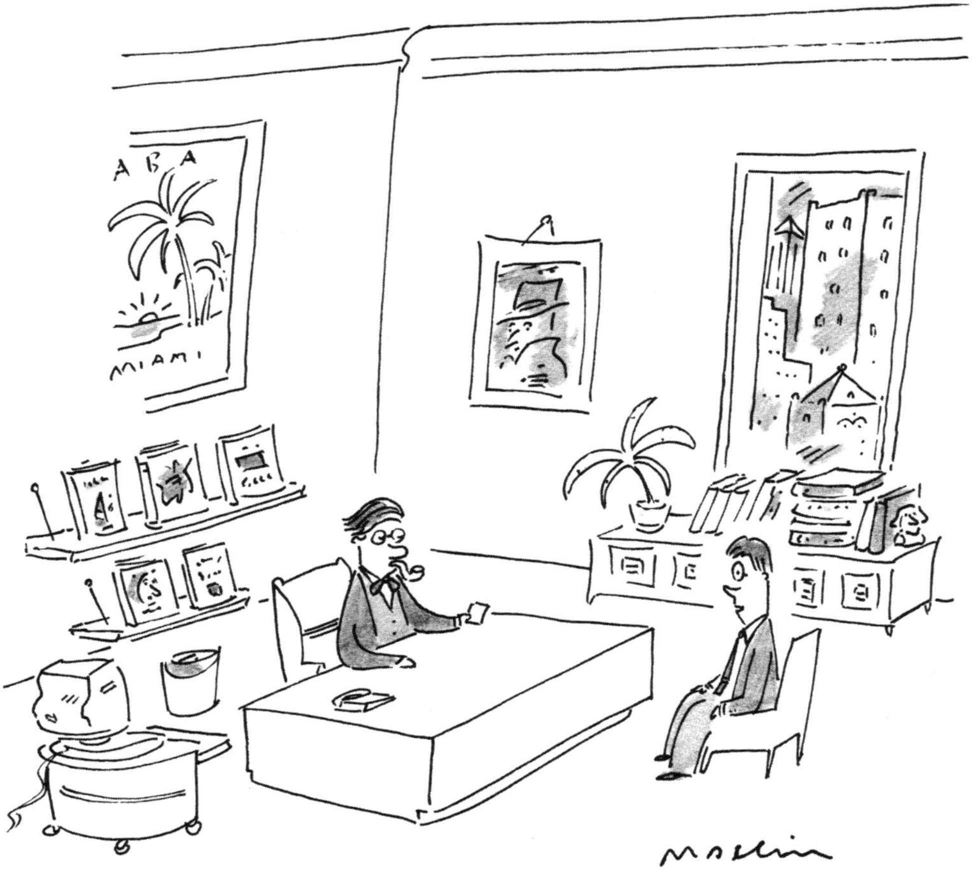
ABA
MIAMI

"I don't have a title yet, or even a subject. All I have is the price: twenty-three ninety-five in hardcover."

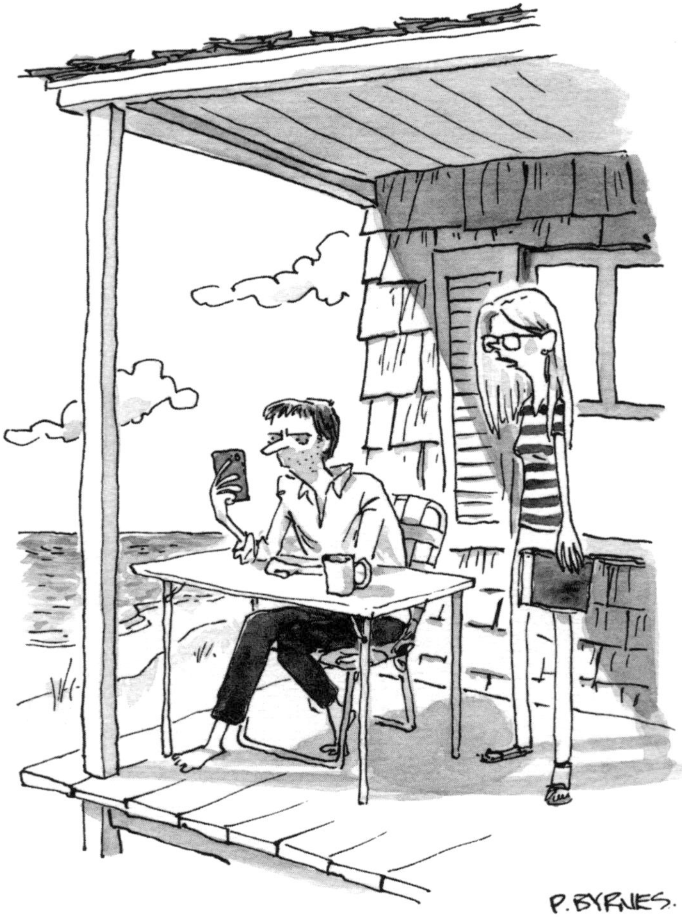
P. BYRNES.

"How goes the Great American Tweet?"

"I'm concerned because your daughter is still reading at a *New York Times* mass-market paperback bestseller level."

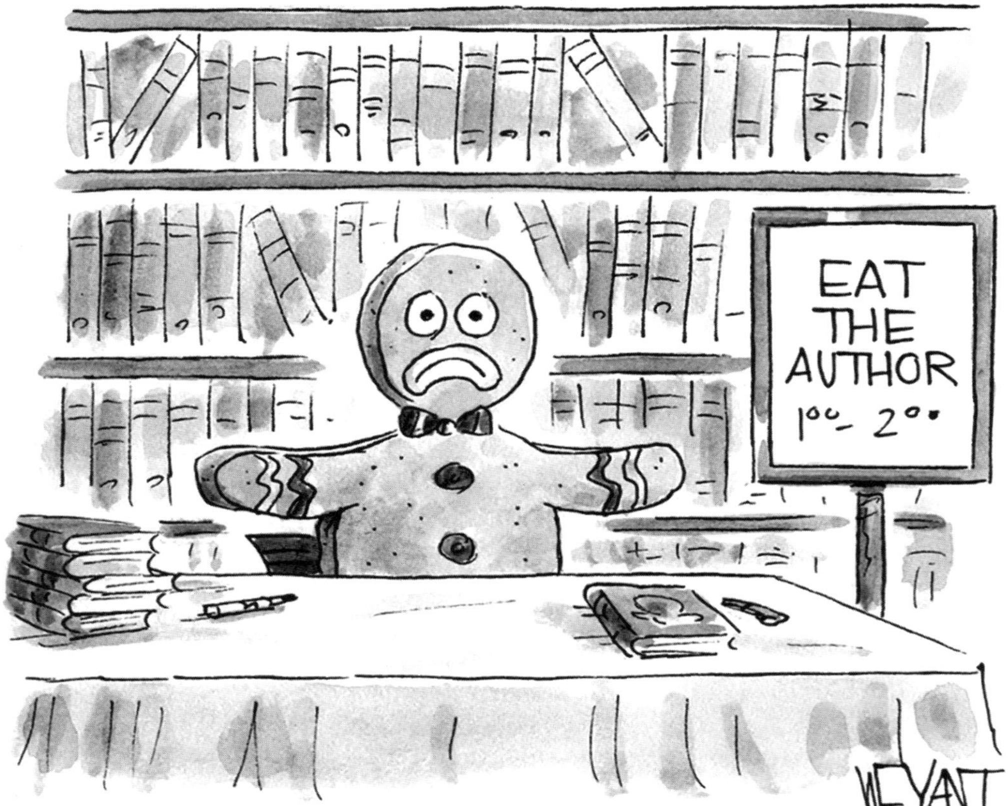
EAT
THE
AUTHOR
1⁰⁰- 2⁰⁰
WEYANT

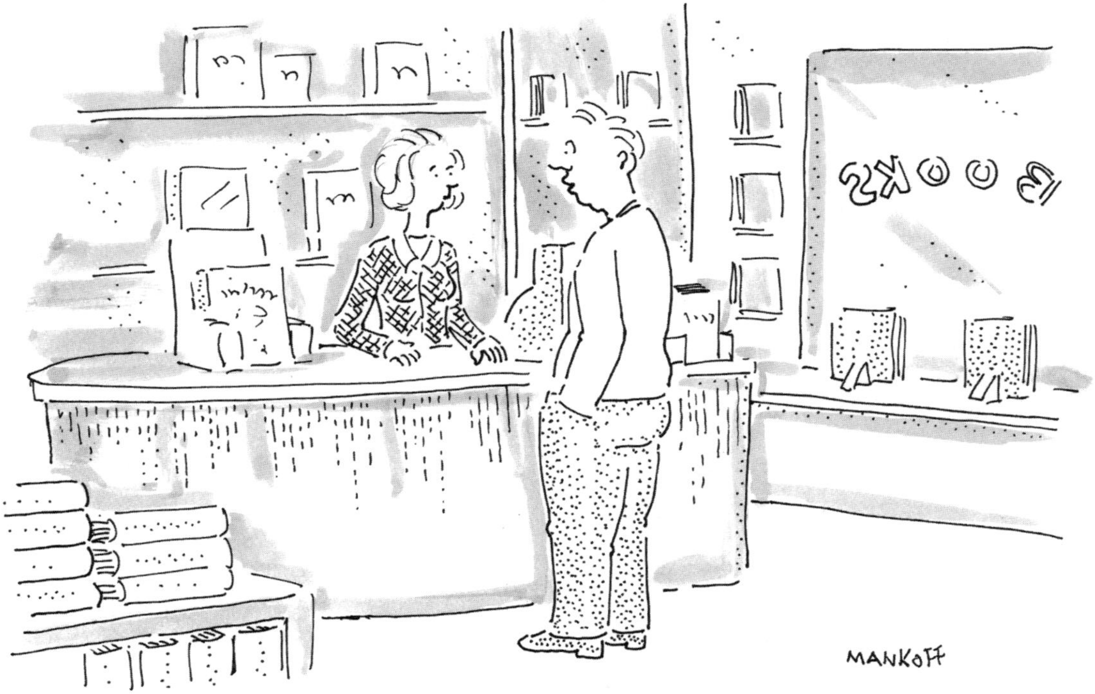
MANKOFF

“Do you have *Intelligence for Idiots*?”

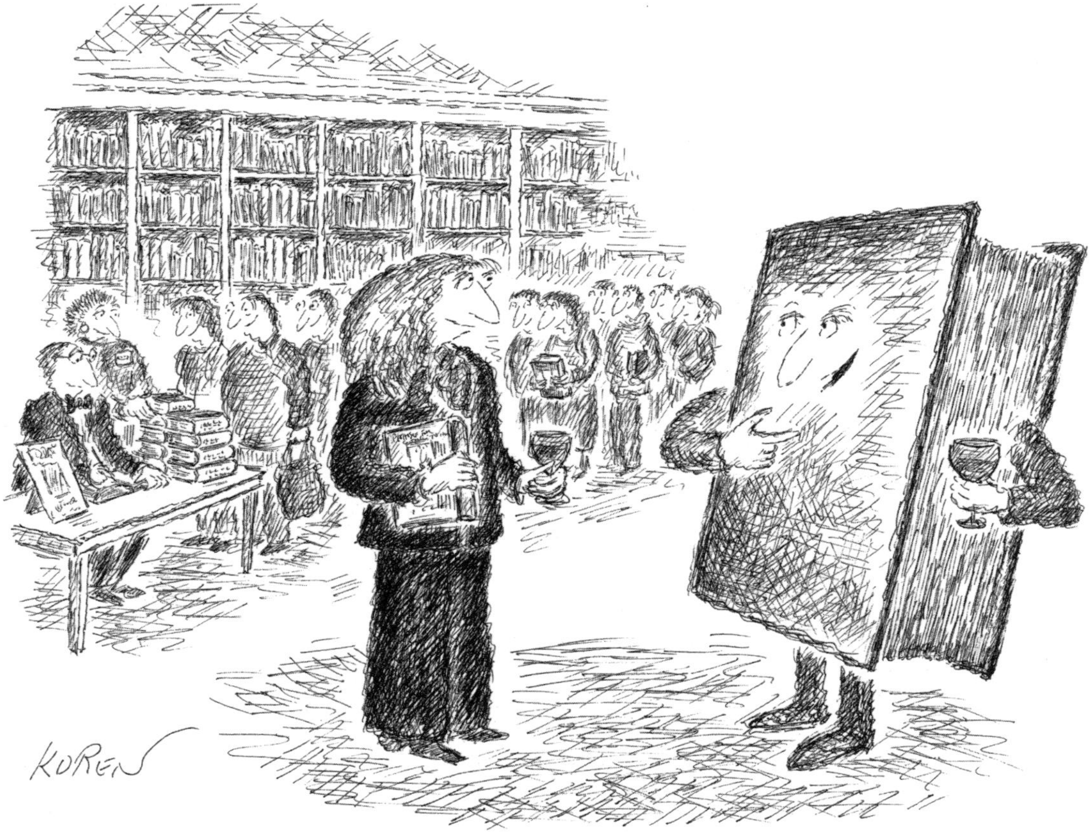
KOREN

"I'm self-published."

"She just graduated from Yale and sold her memoirs—
that's what's bothering me."

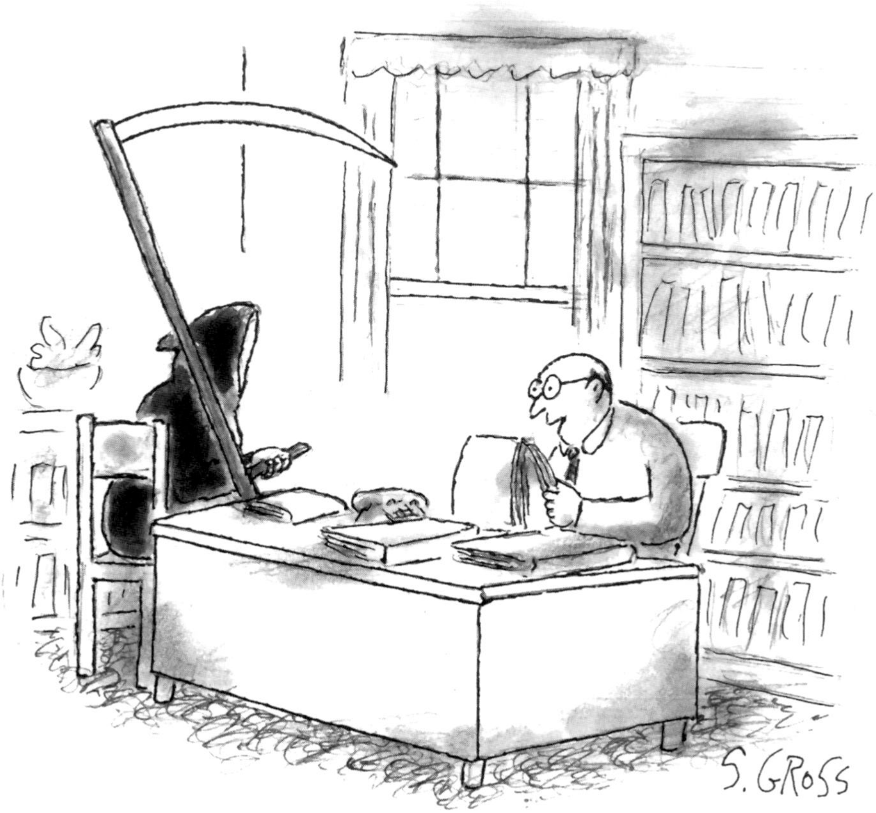
S. GROSS

"By God! This is deathless prose!"

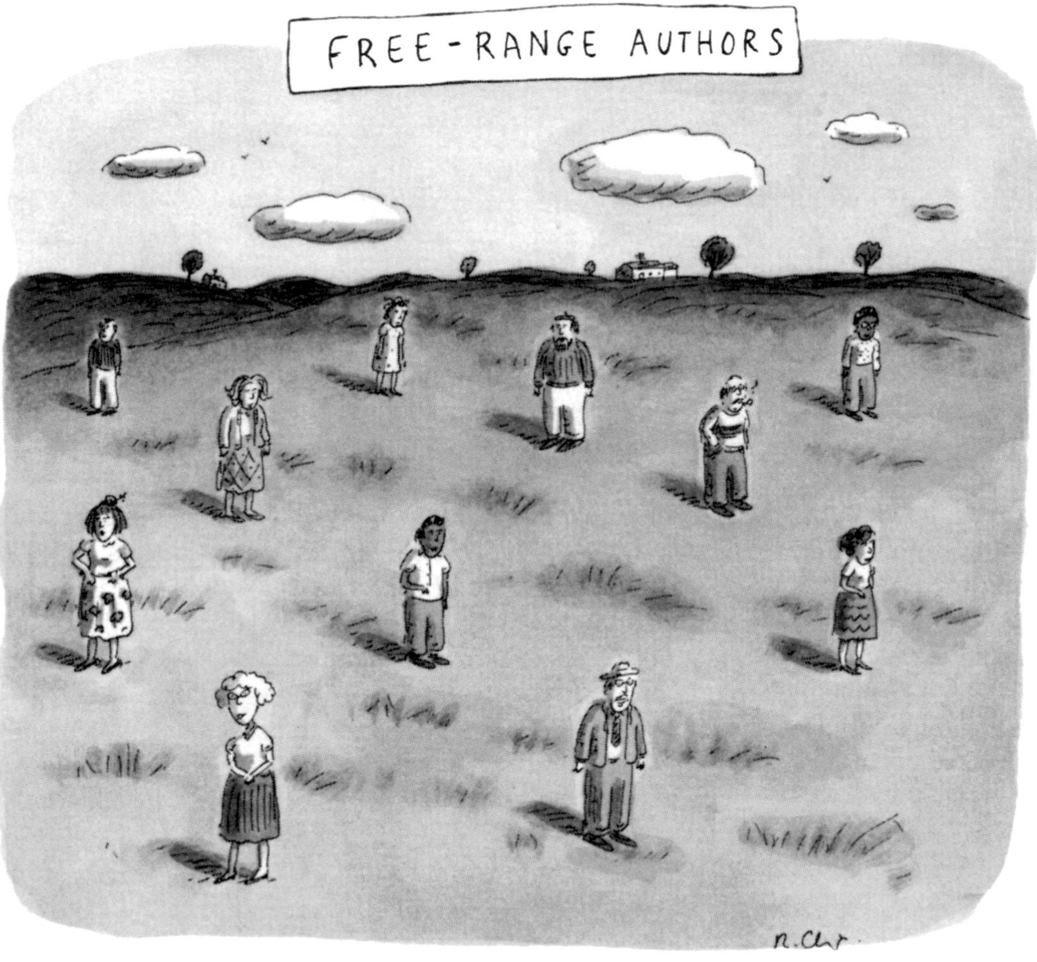
FREE-RANGE AUTHORS

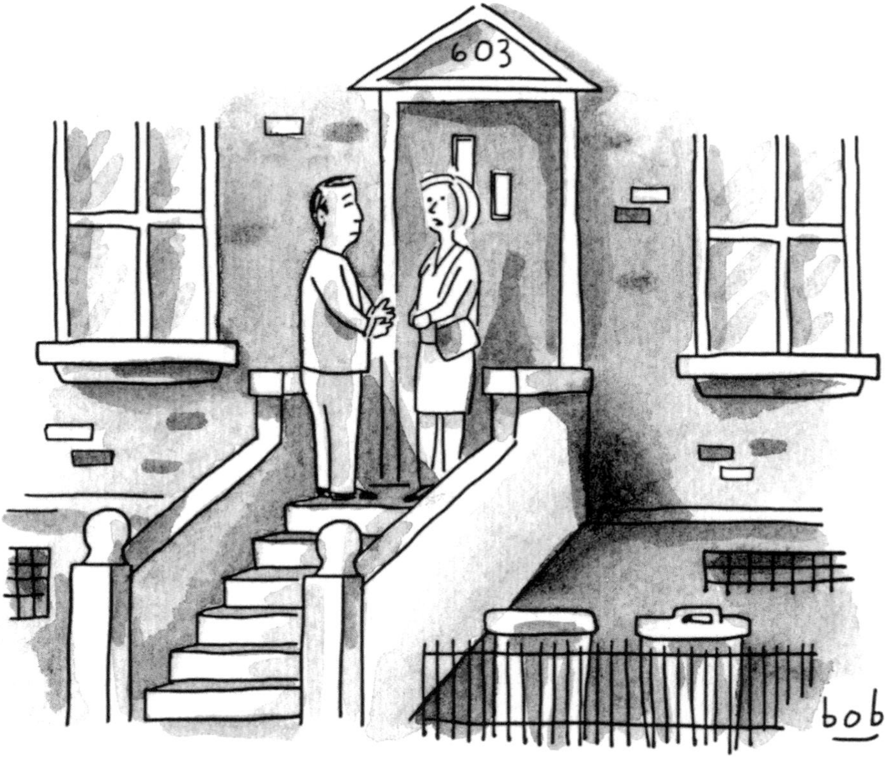
603
bob

"Steve, trust me, this has nothing to do with you being self-published."

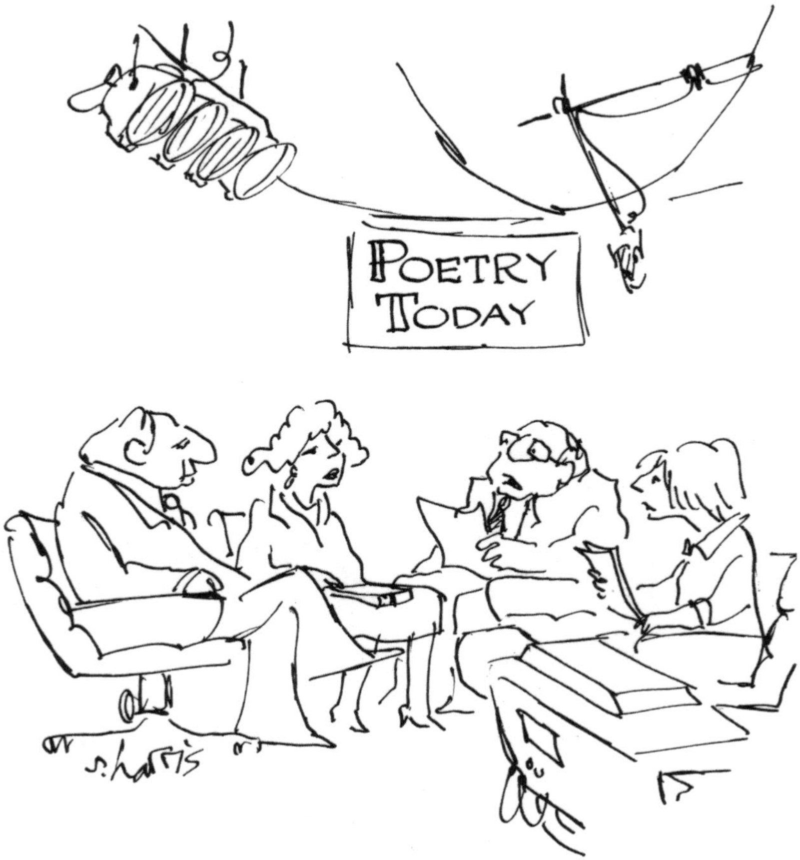
POETRY
TODAY

"Then we're agreed. It *doesn't* have to rhyme."

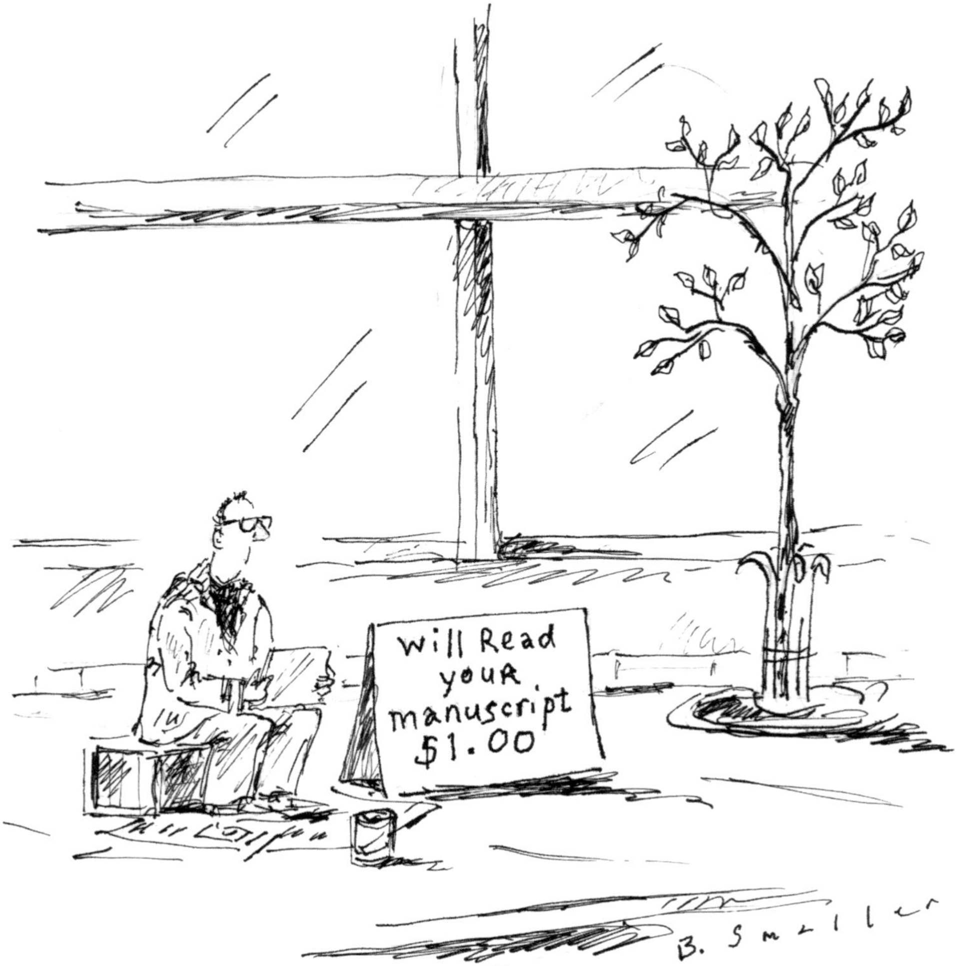
Will Read
your
manuscript
$1.00
B. Smaller

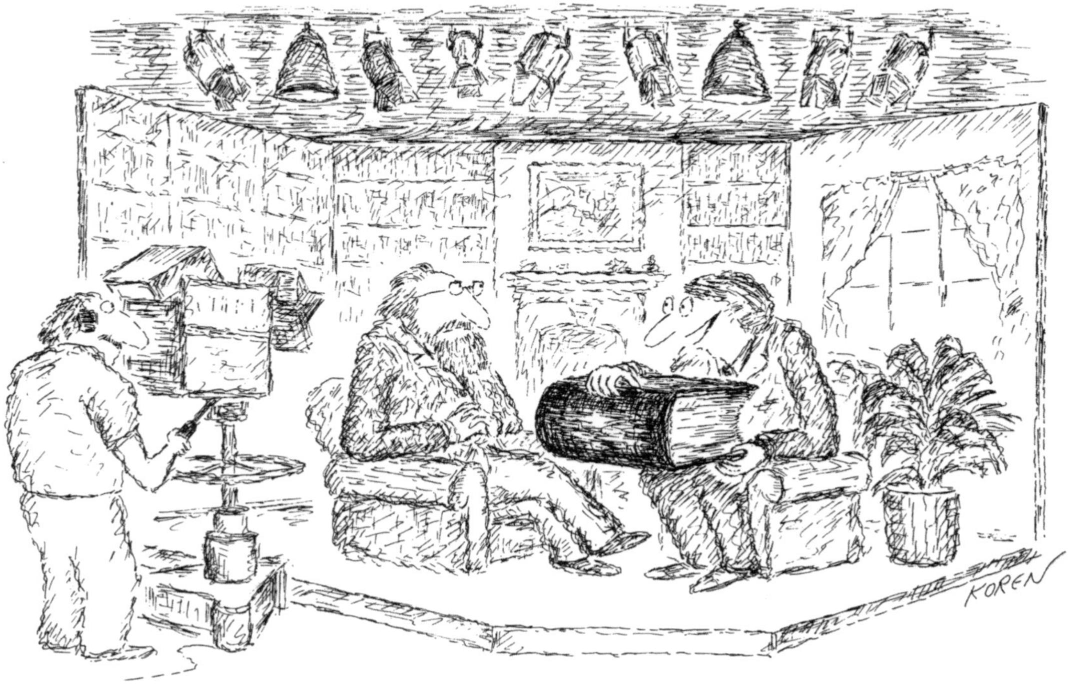
KOREN

"If you were to boil your book down to a few words, what would be its message?"

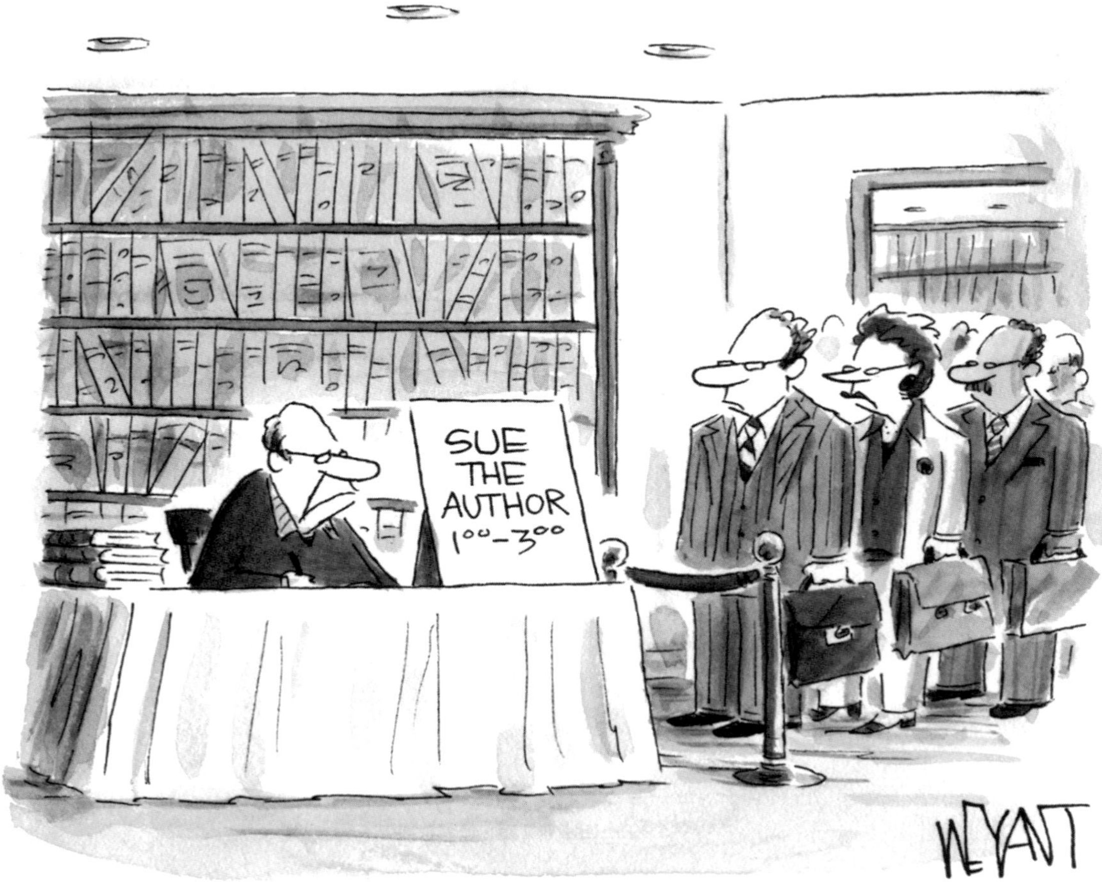
SUE
THE
AUTHOR
1⁰⁰–3⁰⁰
WEYANT

"I hope you all brought books to read."

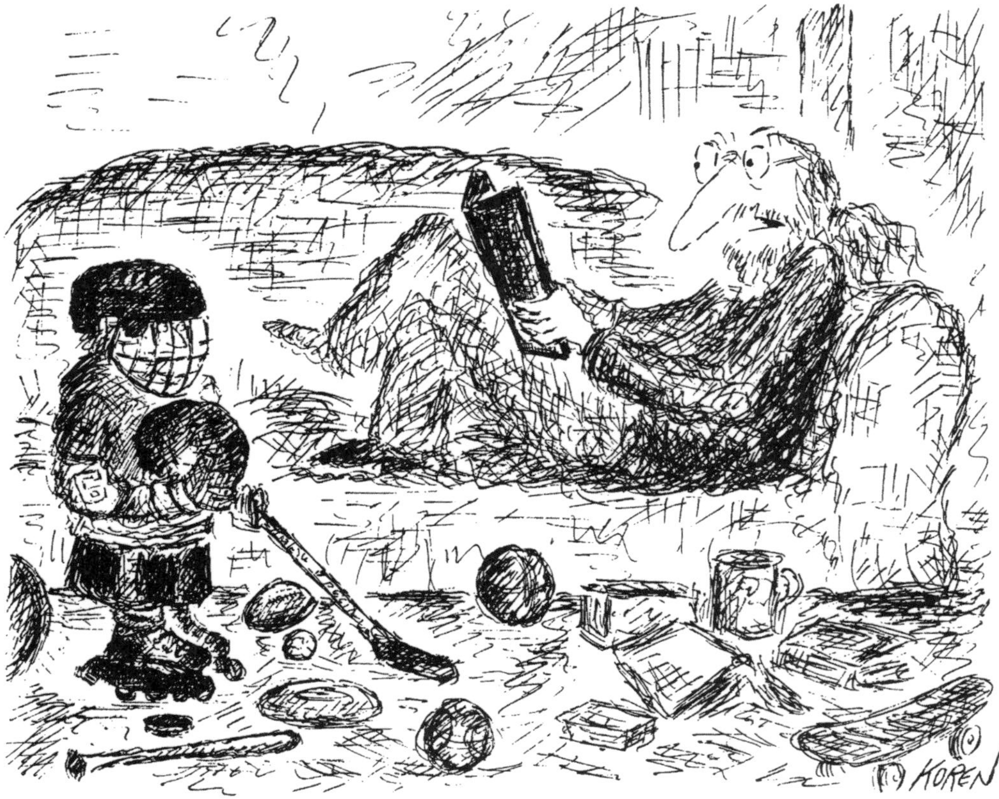
KOREN

"For the last time—Daddy doesn't do sports."

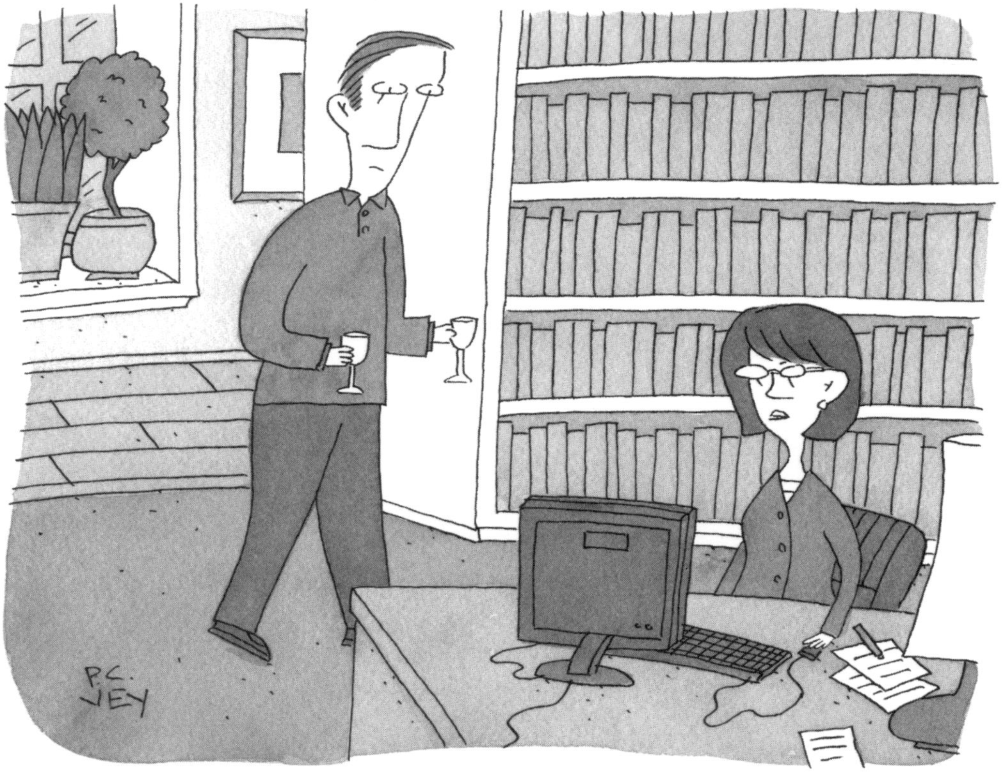
P.C. VEY

"The reviews say I write like somebody who lives with an idiot."

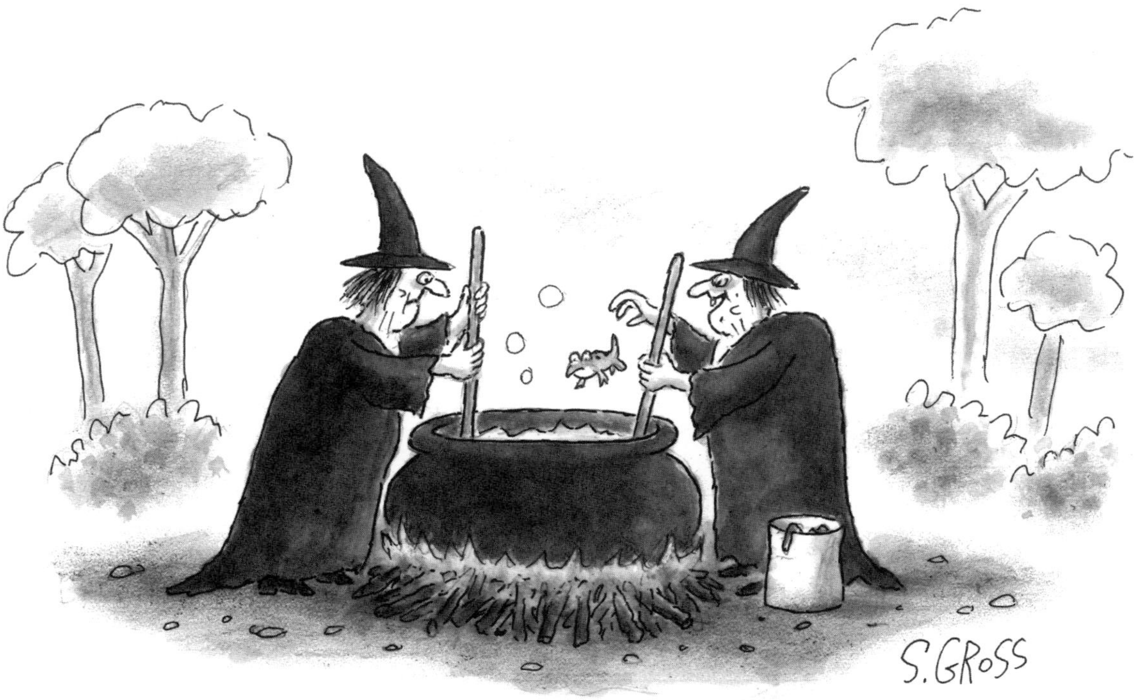
S. GROSS

"I'm writing my memoirs. It's mostly recipes."

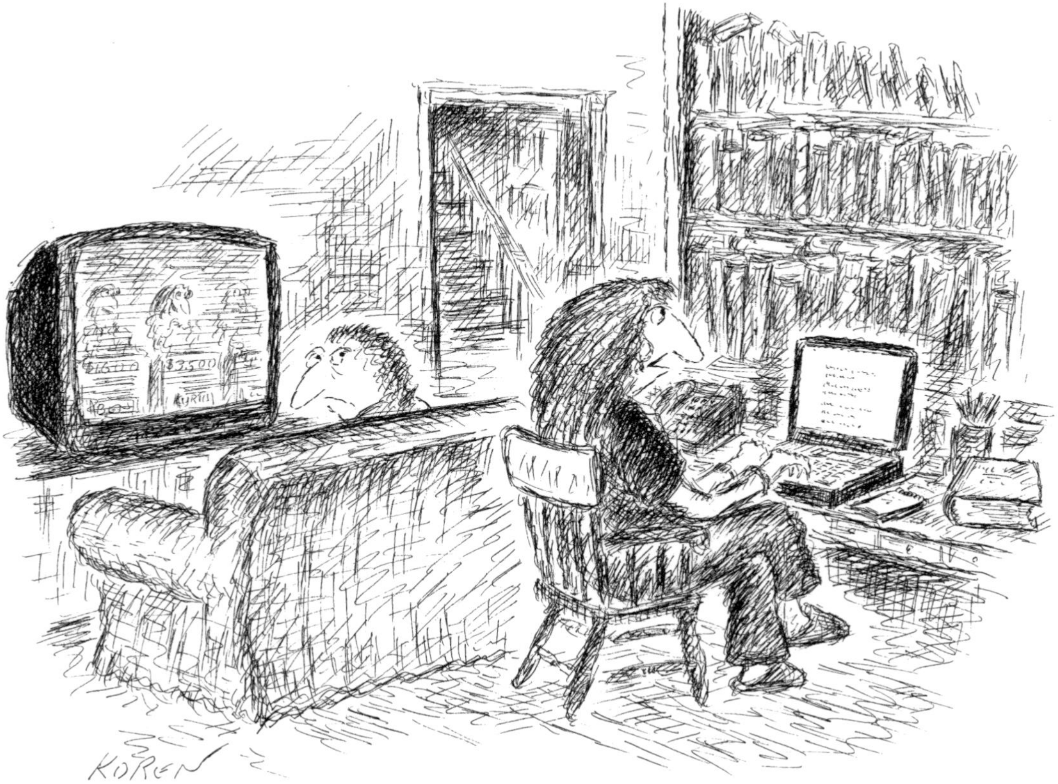
KOREN

"What rhymes with 'failed marriage'?"

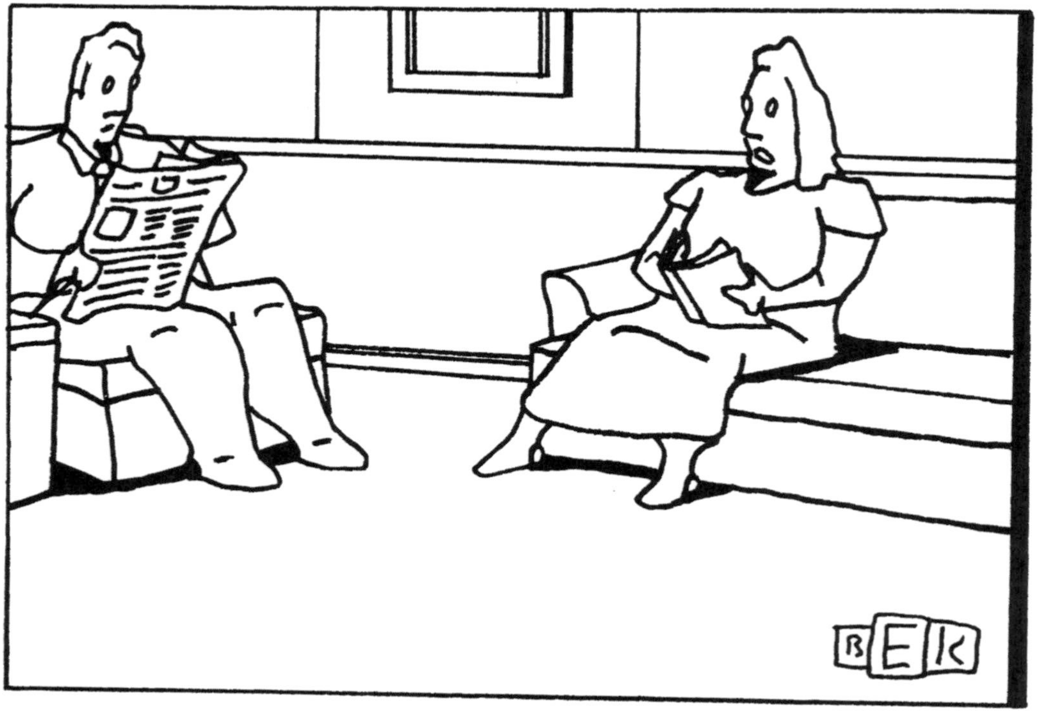
BEK

“Take away his brilliant prose, and he’s just some depressed guy.”

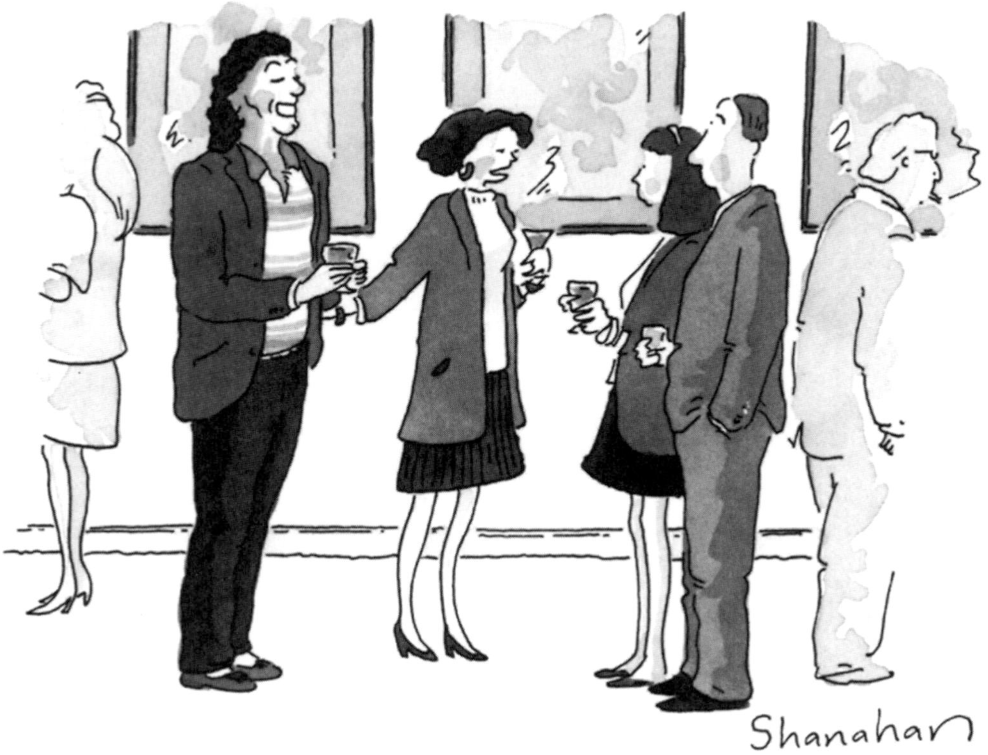
Shanahan

"Peter is completely fictitious, but he's extremely well written."

"I got remaindered."

"I enjoy poetry, but only if it's funny."

"I feel that I have at least one more unpublished novel in me."

BANNED CHILDREN'S BOOKS
MOMMY, WHAT'S A "BURGER" MADE OUT OF?
WAS GRANDMA ALWAYS OLD?
PEOPLE WHO GOT AWAY WITH IT
R. Ch

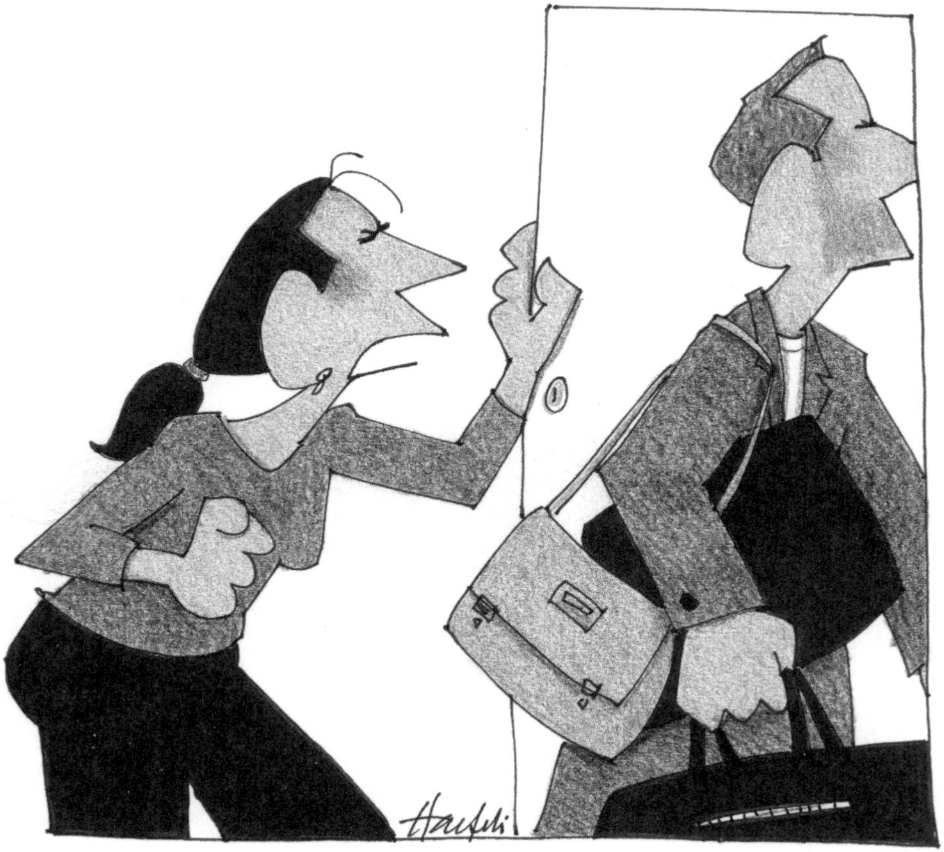

Hauefeli

"I don't need you. I have a book deal."

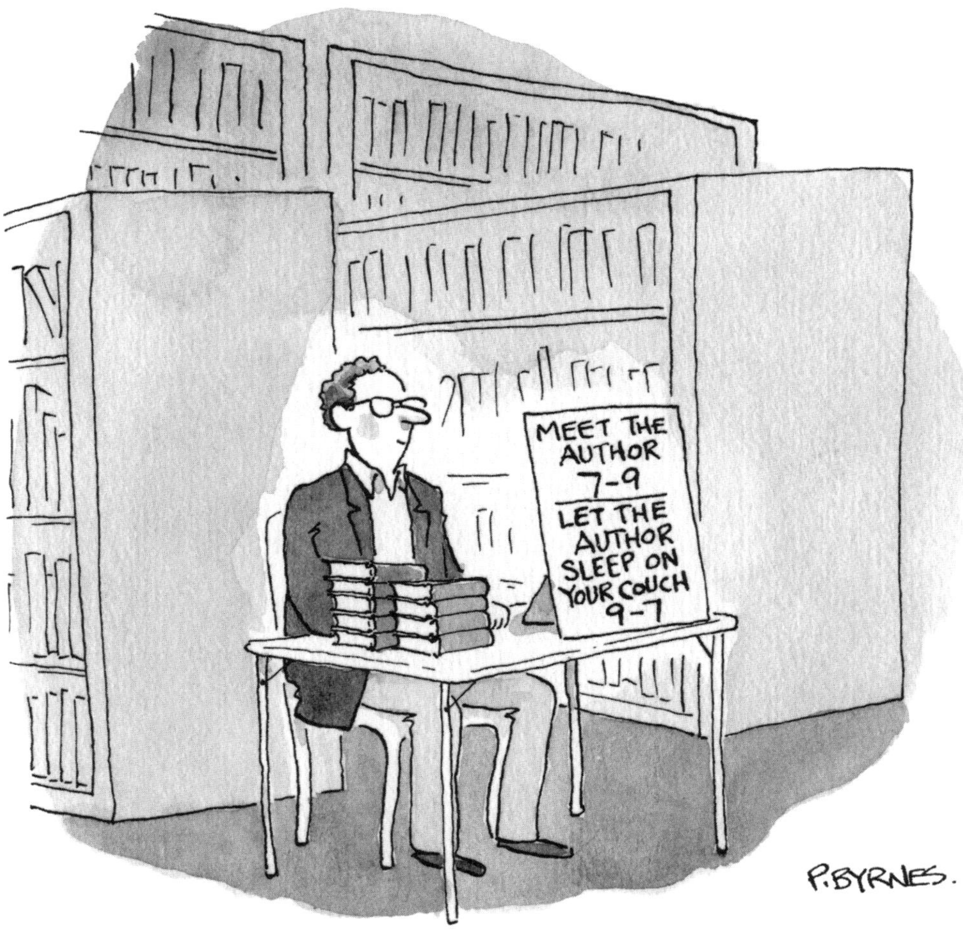
MEET THE AUTHOR 7-9
LET THE AUTHOR SLEEP ON YOUR COUCH 9-7
P. BYRNES.

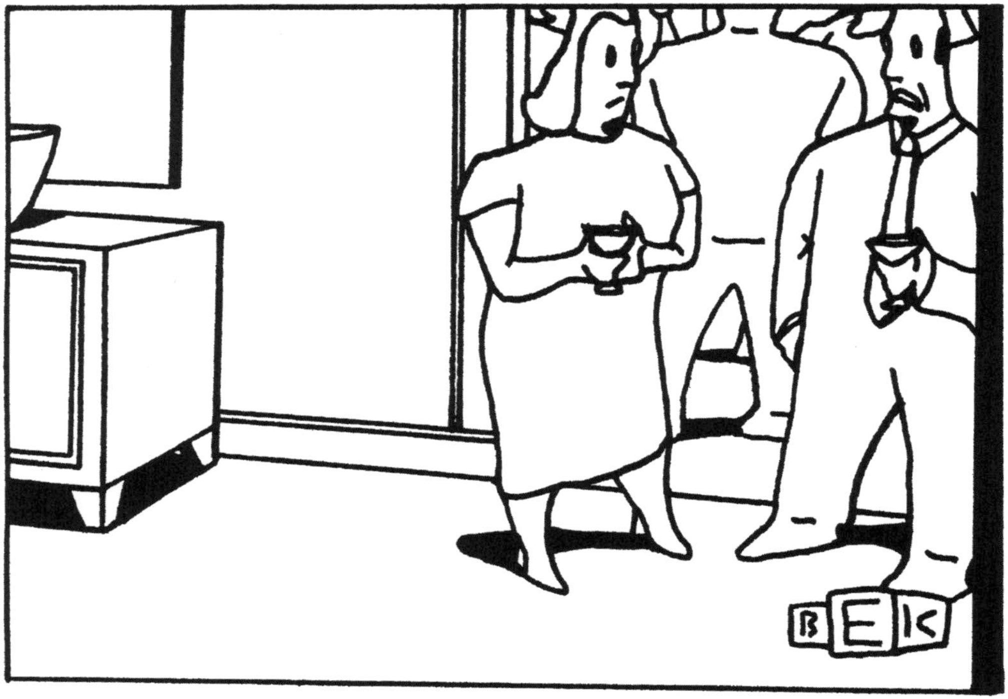
BEK

"It is a tale told by an idiot, full of sound and fury, signifying nothing, and No. 1 on the best-seller list."

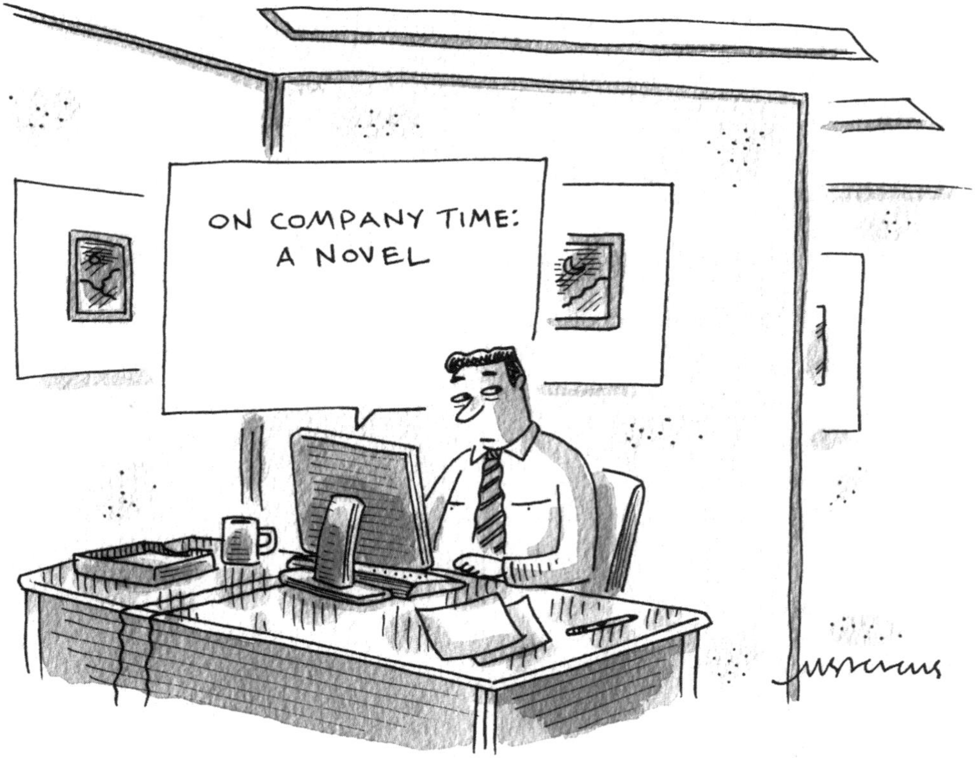
ON COMPANY TIME:
A NOVEL

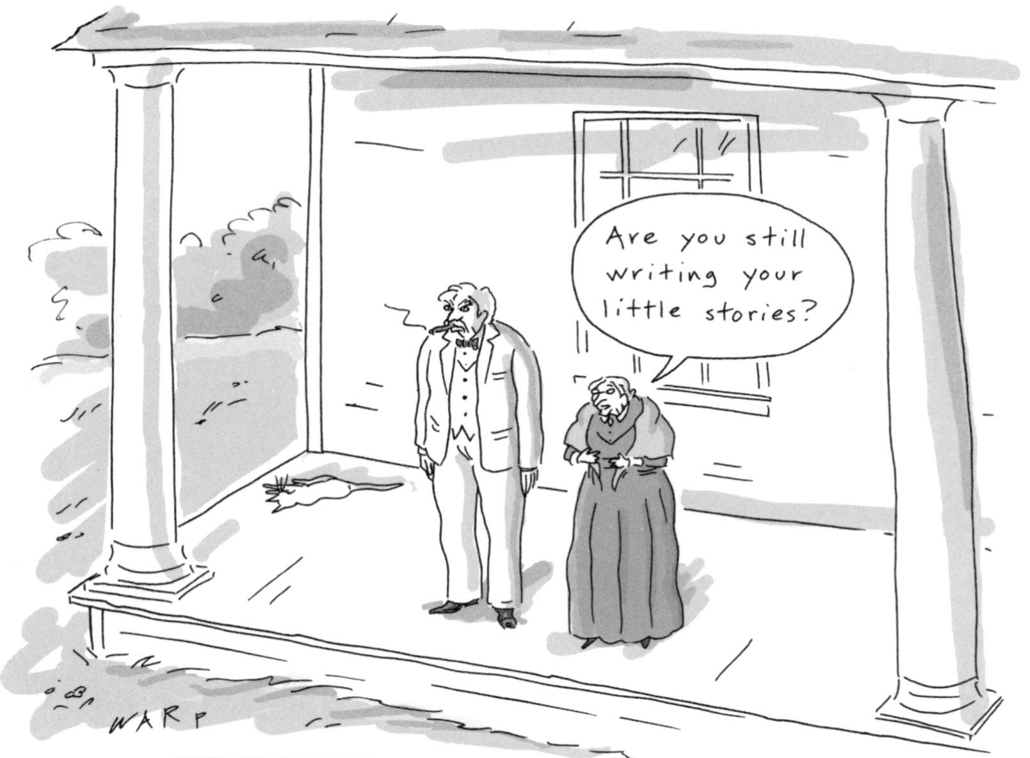
Are you still writing your little stories?
WARP

Mark Twain's Mother

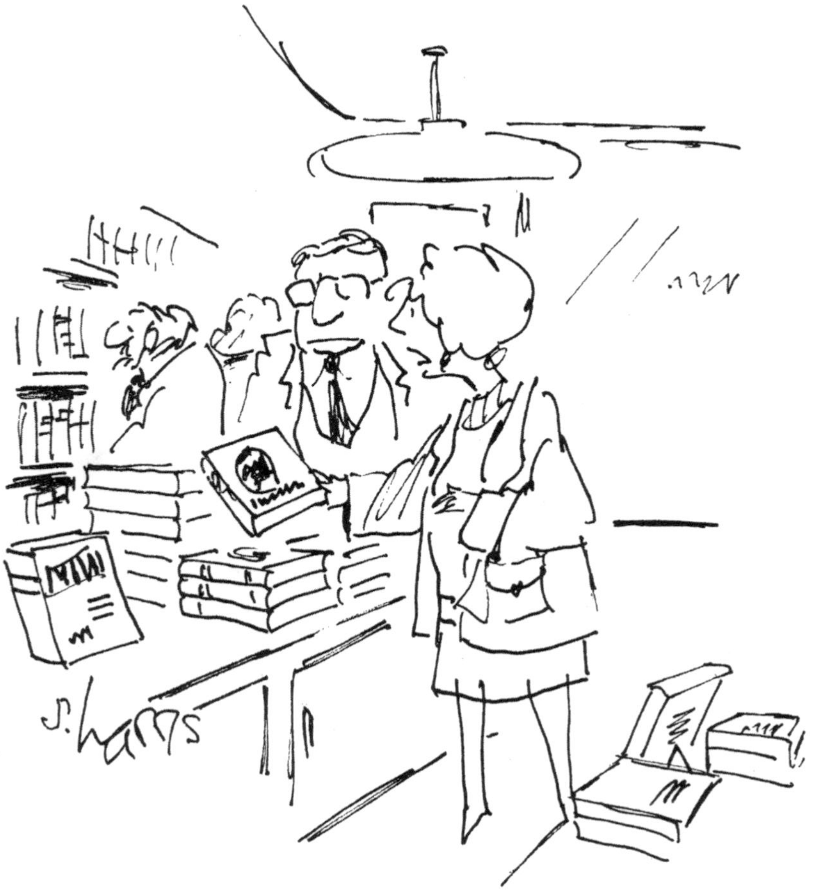
S. Harris

"Let's both read it. Then we'll have something to talk about."

HAMLET vs. AMAZON PRIME
To buy, or not to buy, that is the question.
Definitely nobler to shop locally.
And yet: FREE SHIPPING.
R. Chast

"I'm trying to catch up on my beach reading."

"How can anyone expect me to write with this constant crashing of the waves?"

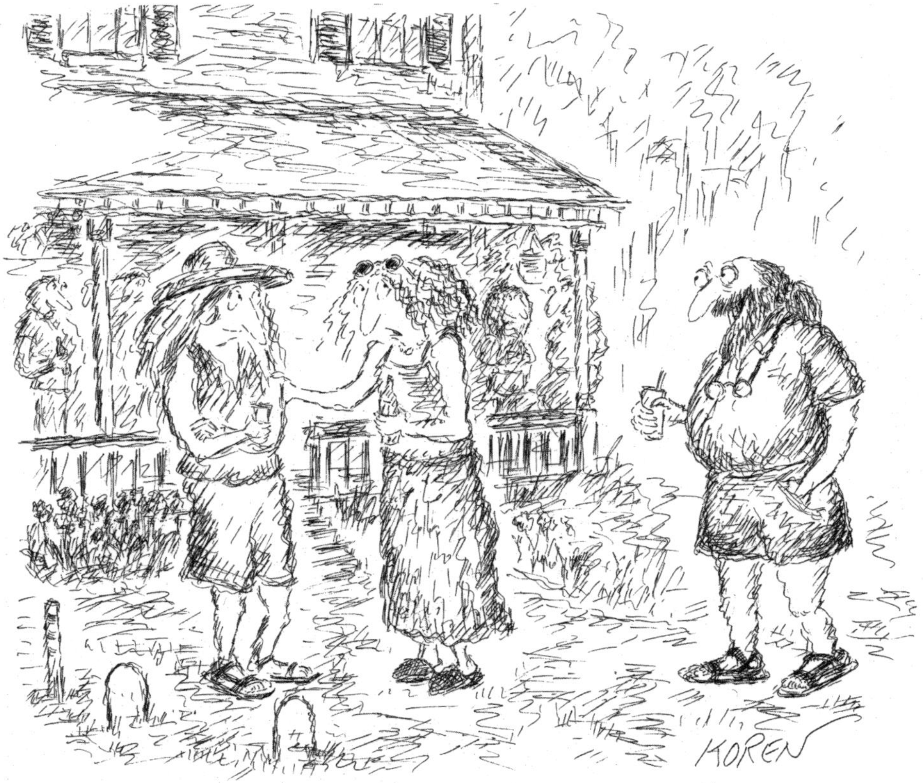
KOREN

“Here comes an out-of-print collection of short stories.”

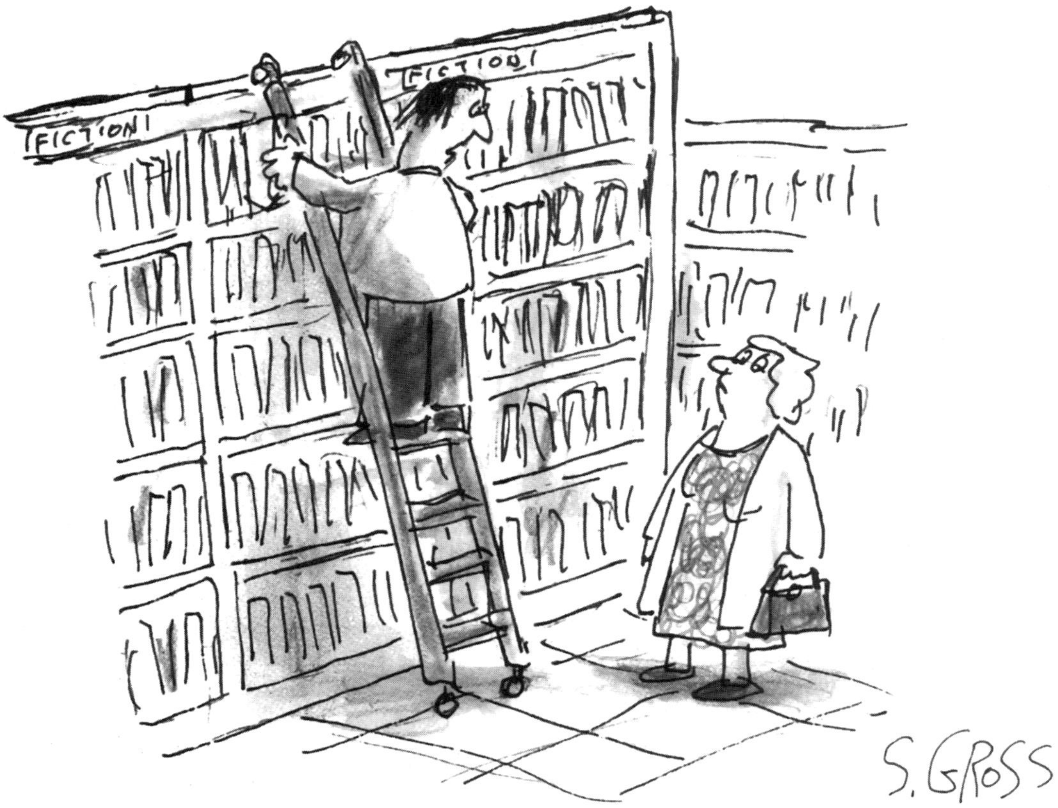
FICTION
FICTION
S. GROSS

"With or without zombies?"

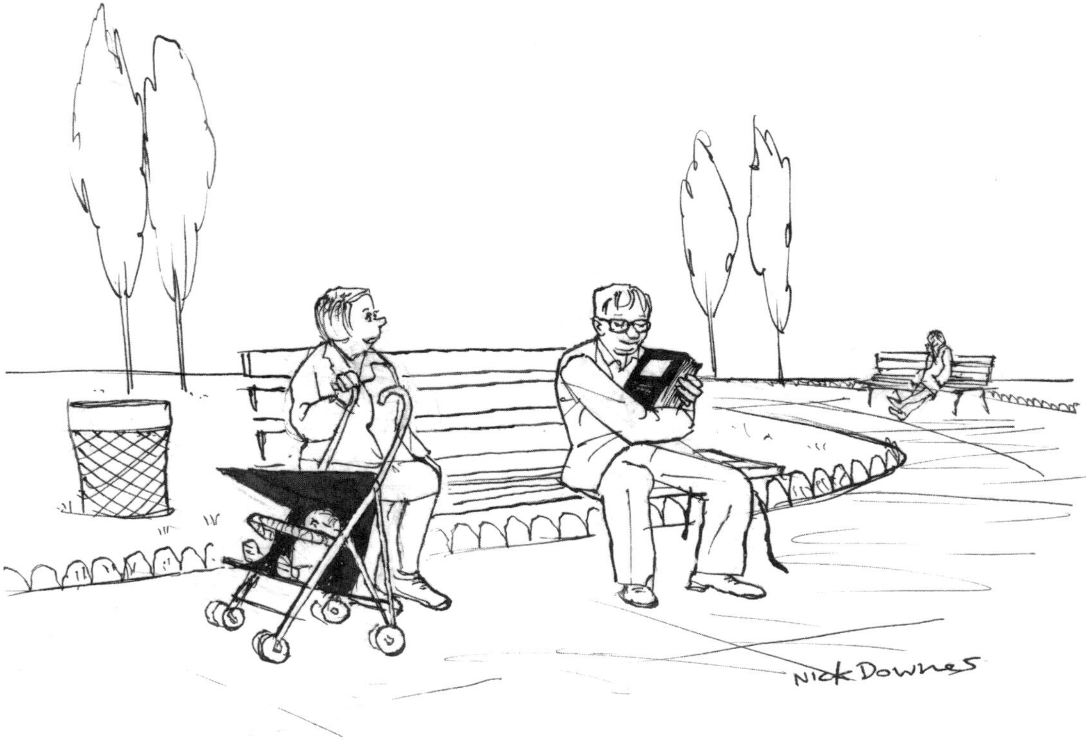
NICK DOWNES

"Your first novel?"

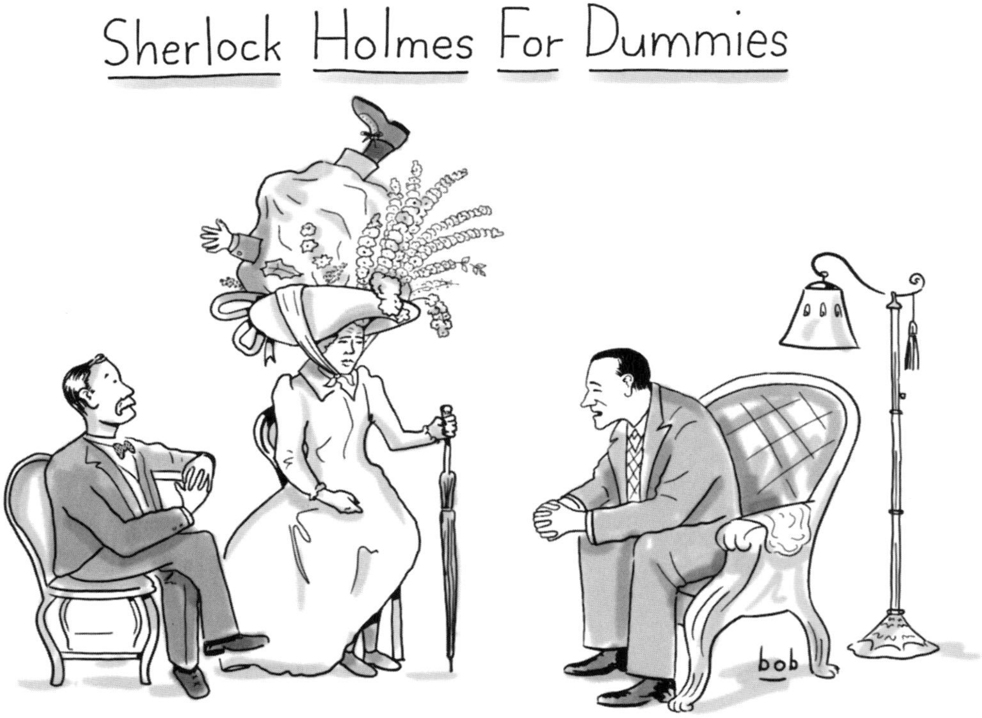
Sherlock Holmes For Dummies
bob

"Lady Fowler, how long has your husband been missing?"

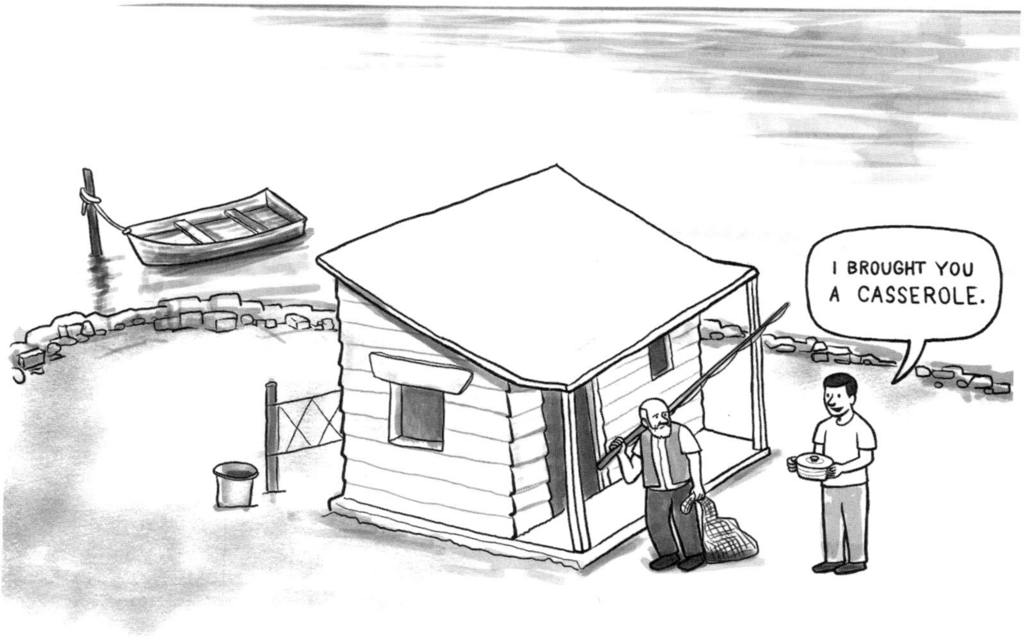
I BROUGHT YOU A CASSEROLE.

THE OLD MAN, THE SEA, AND THE WELL-MEANING NEIGHBOR

PAUL NOTH

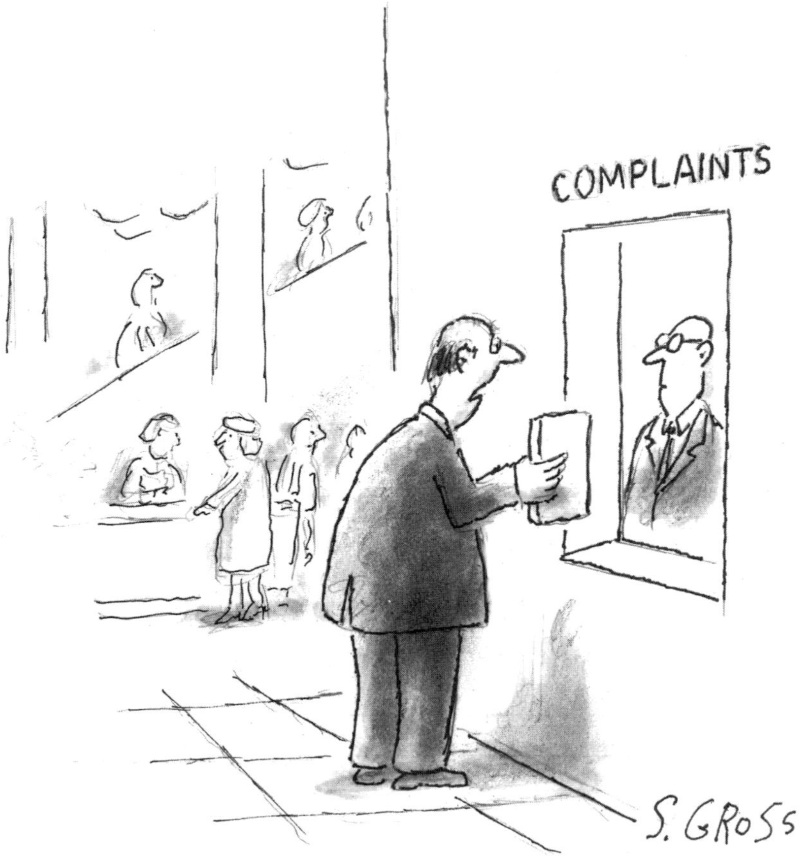
COMPLAINTS
S. GROSS

“This interactive book called me ‘stupid’!”

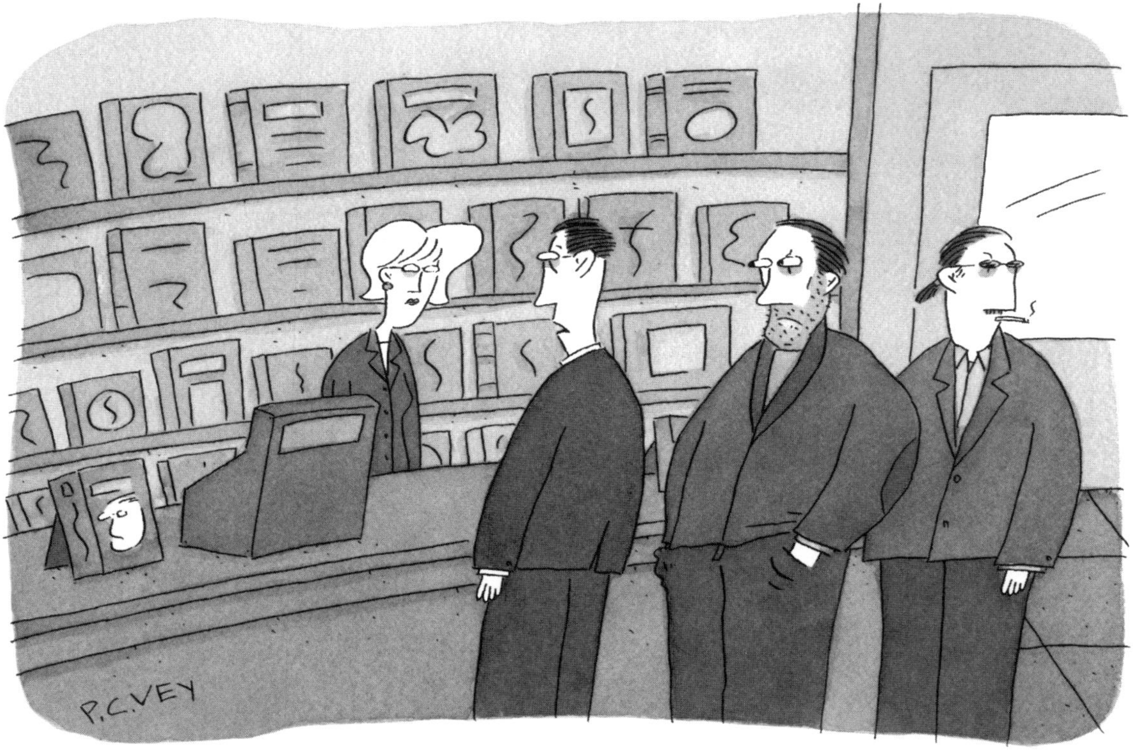
P.C.VEY

"I'm looking for something I can read while stuffed into the trunk of an El Dorado."

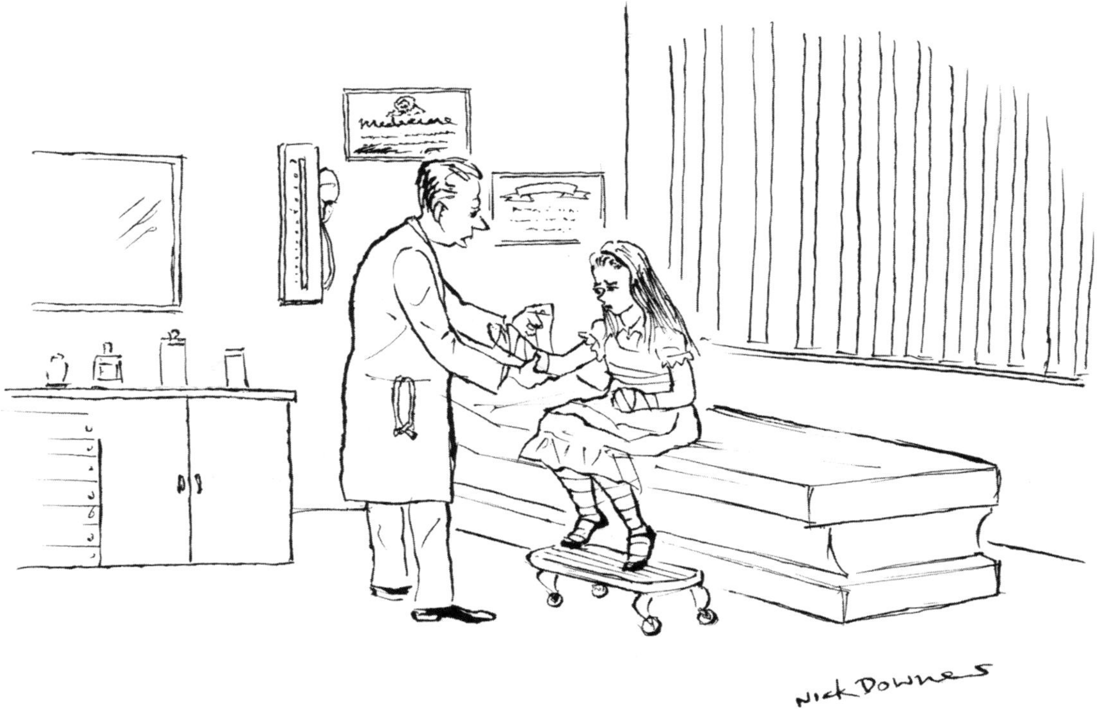
NICK DOWNES

“And no more walking through mirrors, young lady.”

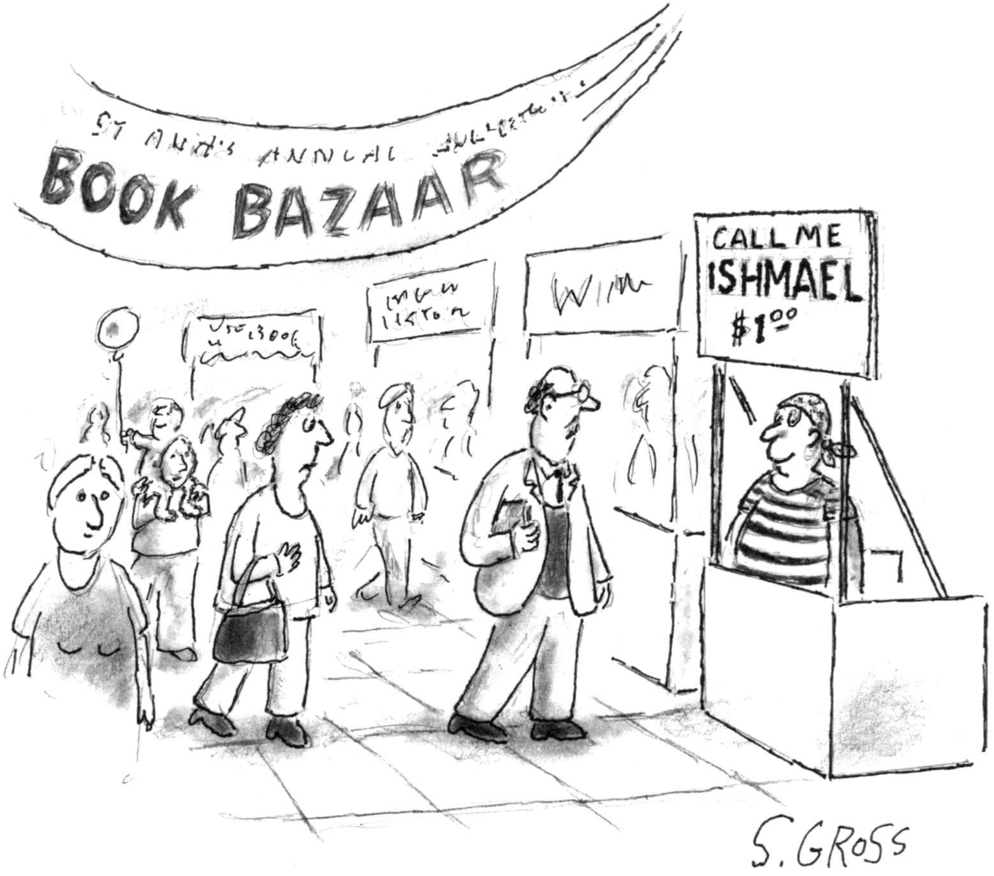
BOOK BAZAAR
CALL ME
ISHMAEL
$1.00
S. GROSS

"Give me a shout if either of you catch sight of the white whale, boys.
I'm going below to check out the ice skating."

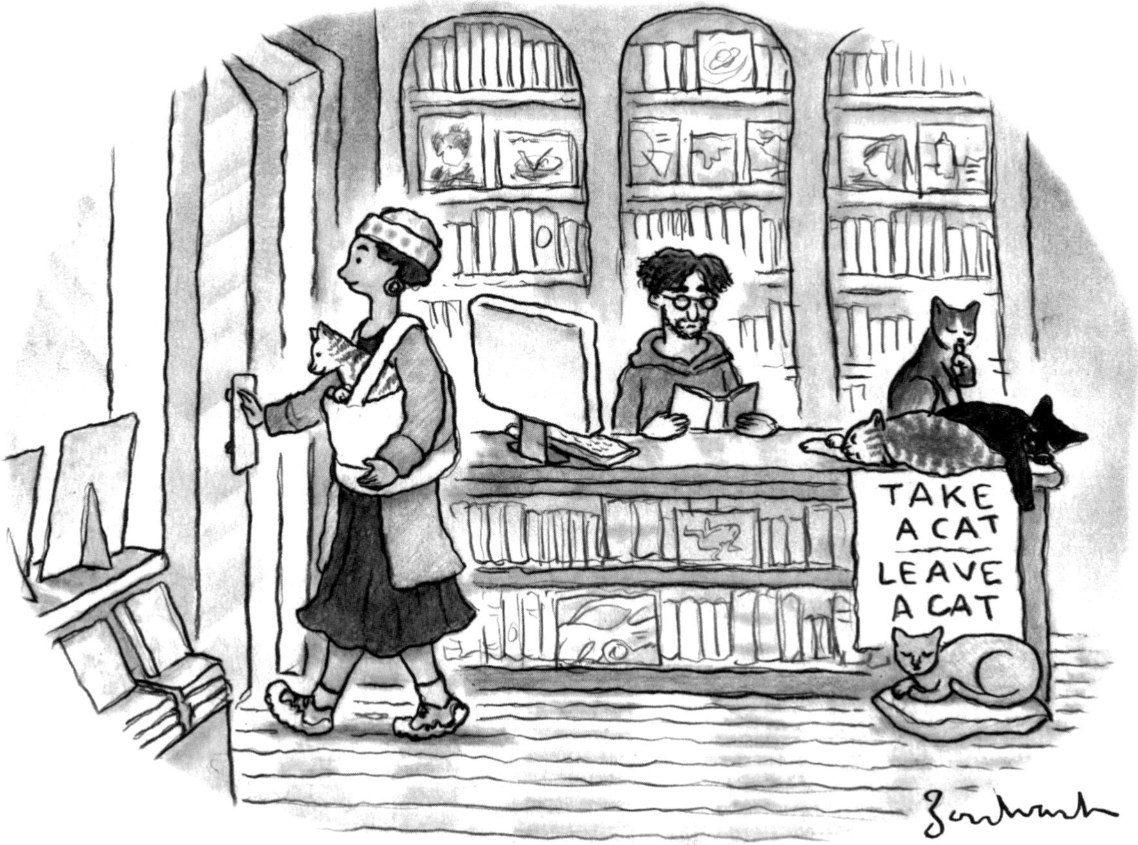
TAKE
A CAT
LEAVE
A CAT

"The editor who turned down the first Harry Potter book, say hello to the publisher who took a pass on Stephen King."

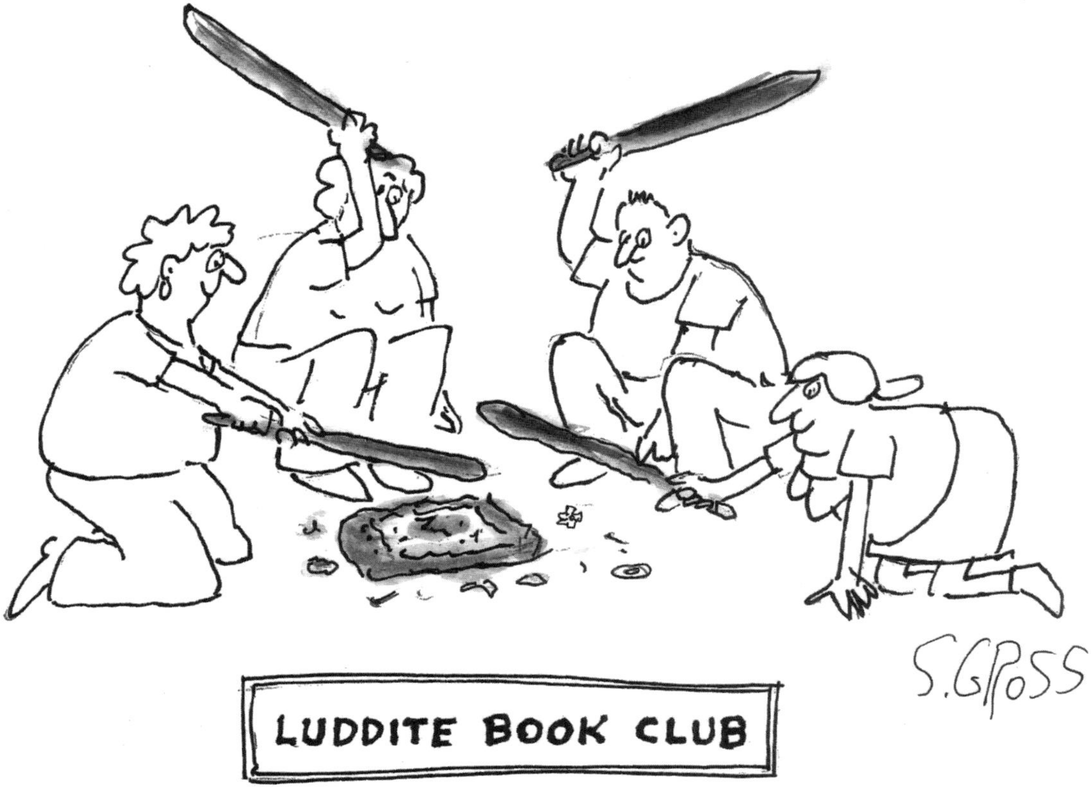
S. GROSS
LUDDITE BOOK CLUB

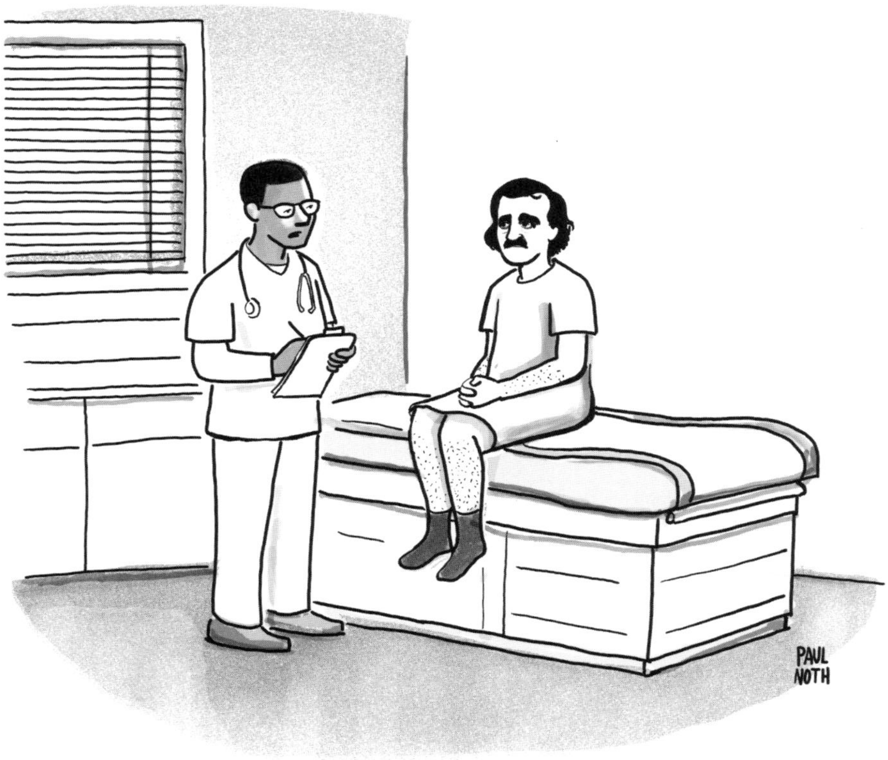
PAUL NOTH

"Your heart rate's good, but it shouldn't be beating under the floor like that."

"GONE WITH THE WIND": THE BEACH BLANKET

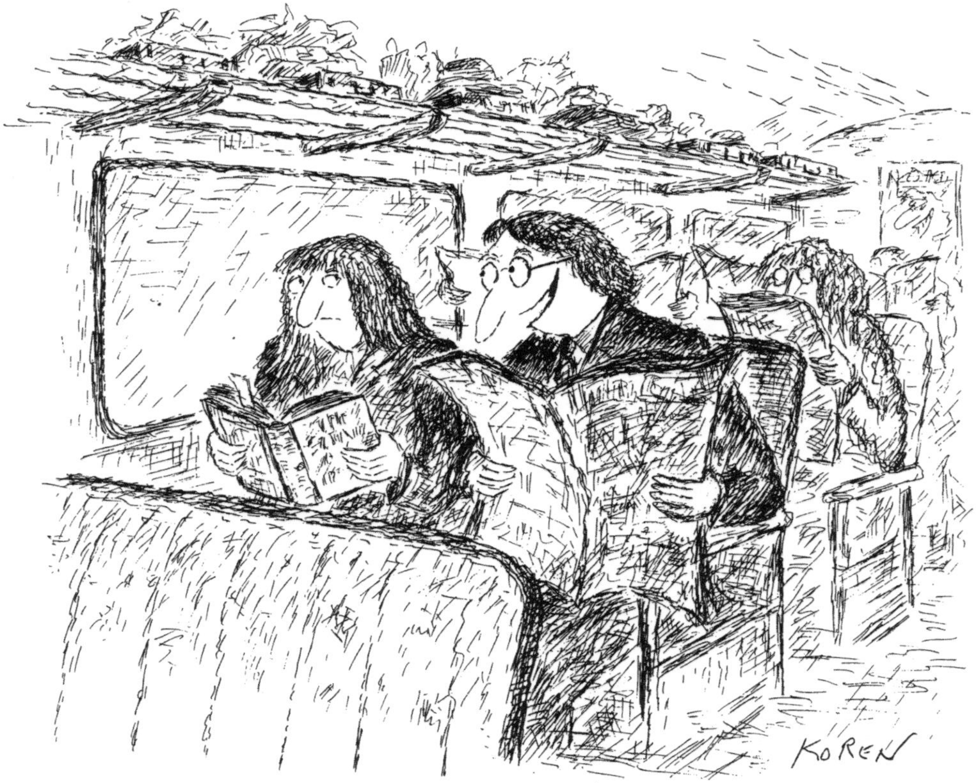
KOREN

“Hemingway! Is he any good?”

```
the sky wassxxxxxxxbigxxxmexxxxx
    wasxdeepxxxmxxxxxy wasxxxxxxxxxxx
    wasxvery nice to look at
    veryxxxxxxxxx azure superb
    shimmered inxthe wasxxxxxgoodx
was beyond description.
```

"Hide in the closet! There's no time to choose something to read in there!"

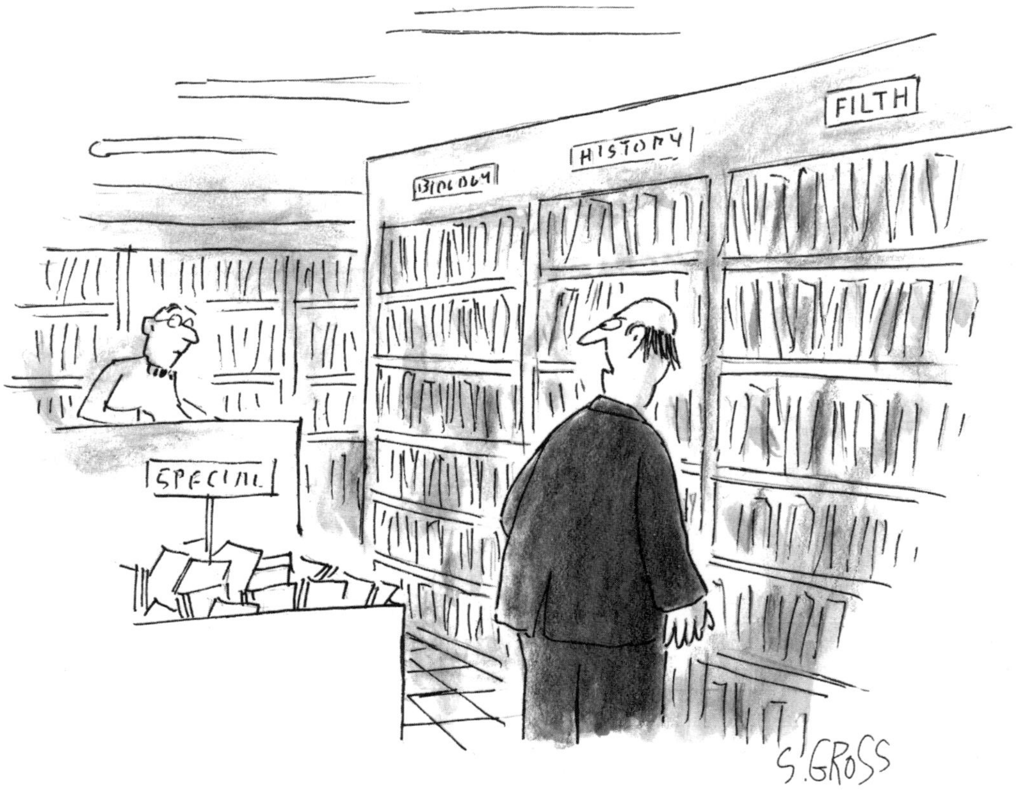
FILTH
HISTORY
BIOLOGY
SPECIAL
S. GROSS

"What happened to 'Erotica'?"

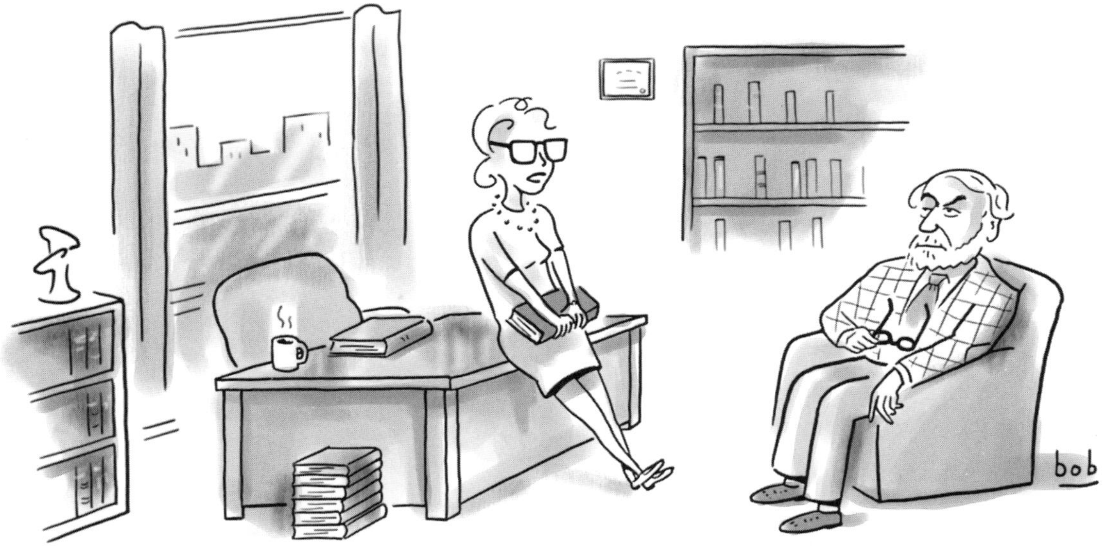
bob

"Can you rewrite this as a coloring book?"

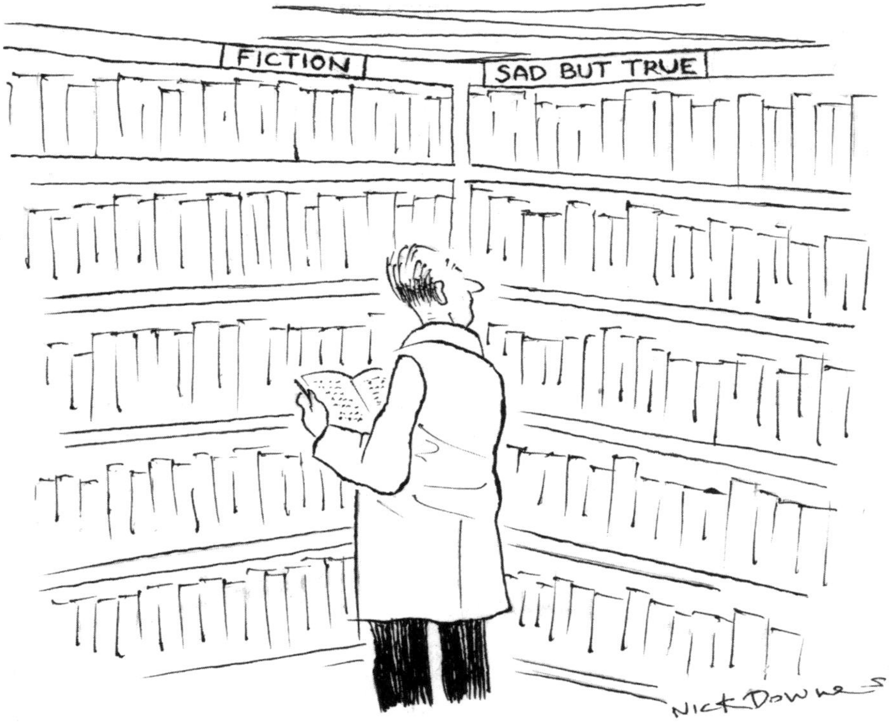
FICTION
SAD BUT TRUE

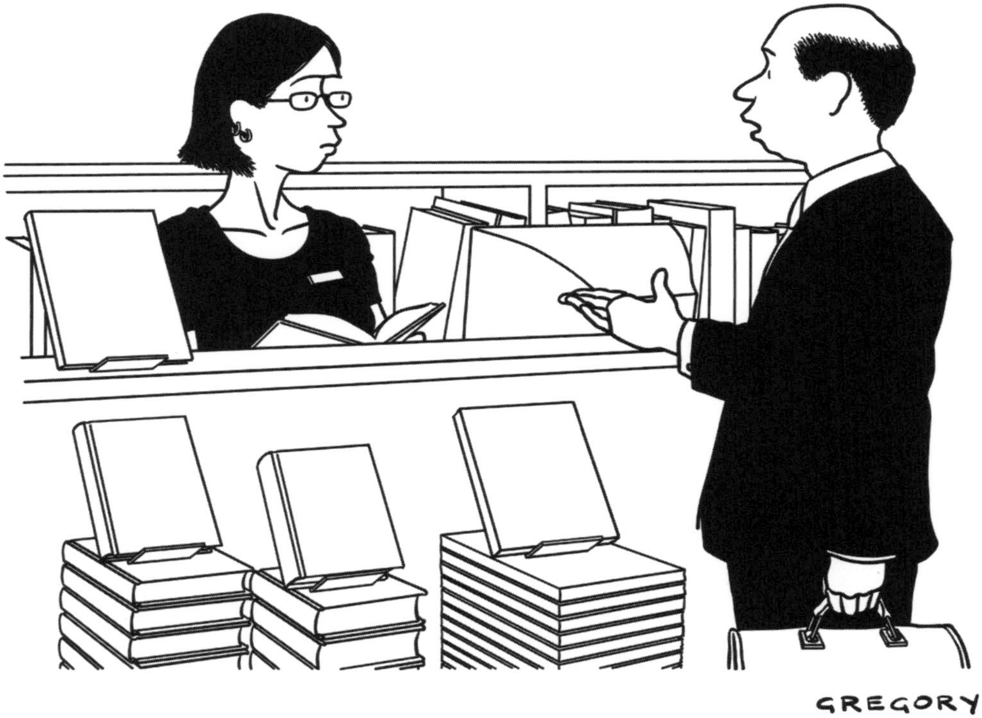
GREGORY

"Do you have any picture books that could help a child understand tort reform?"

"The people in my new novel have started rejecting print media. That's a bad omen."

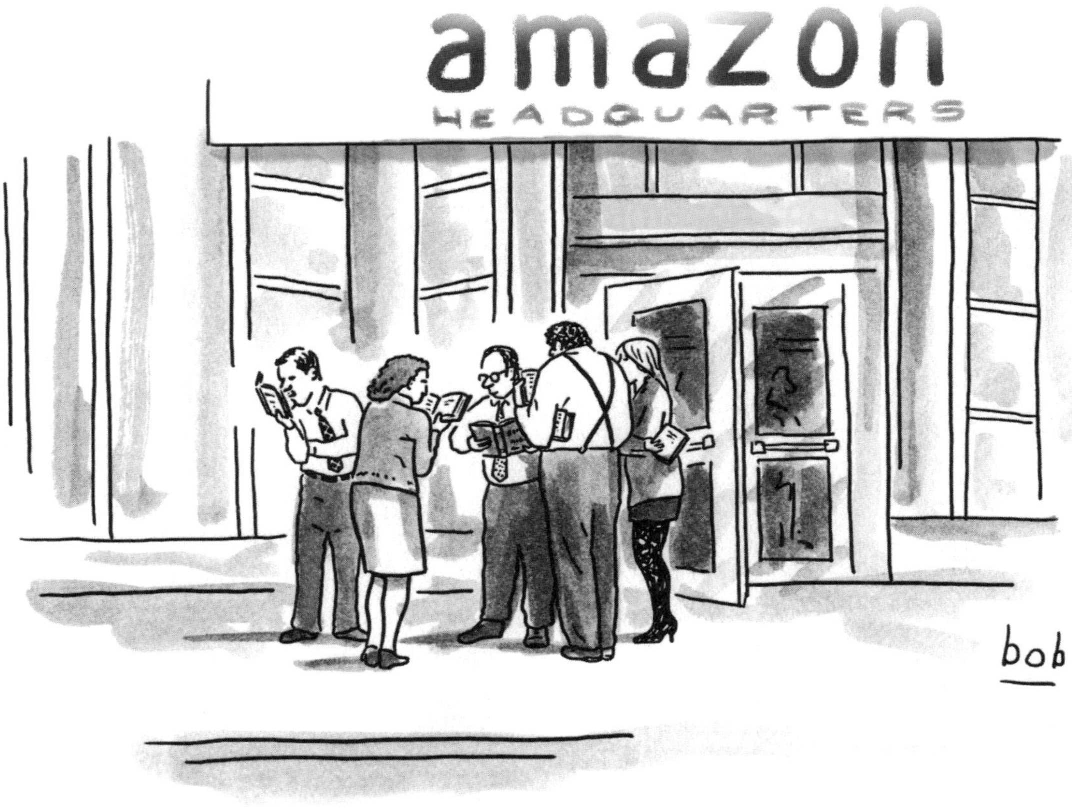
amazon
HEADQUARTERS
bob

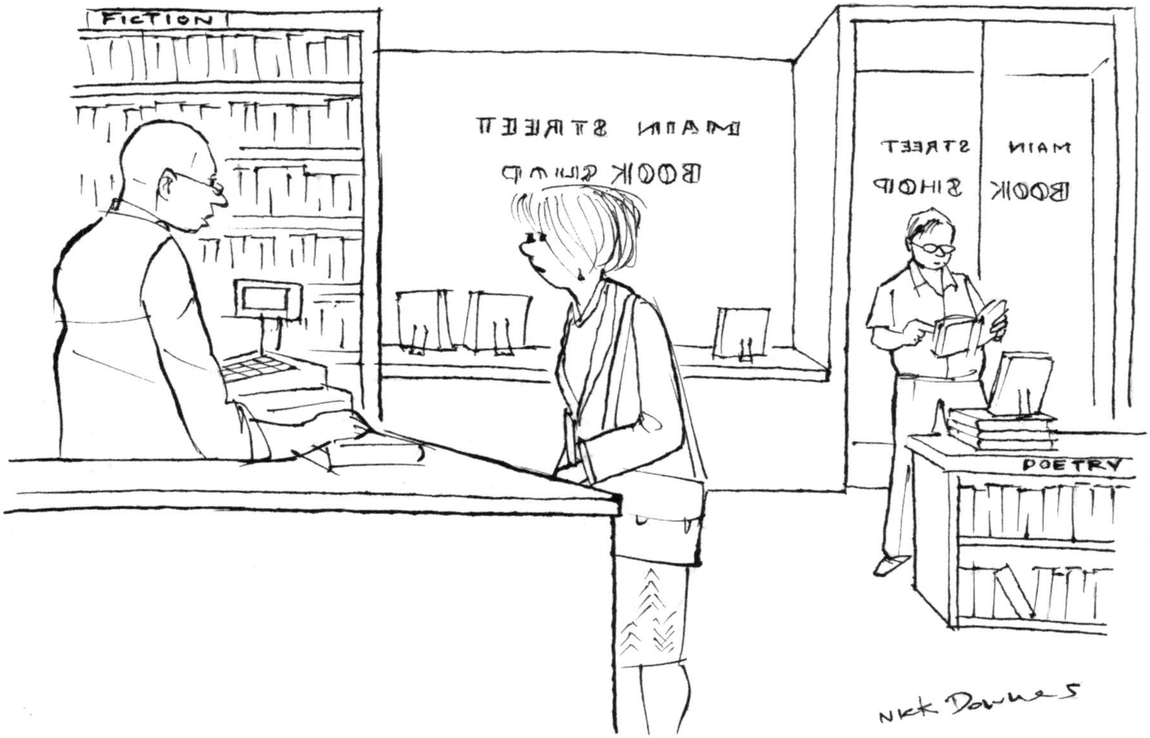
FICTION
POETRY

"Love and marriage are in two separate sections."

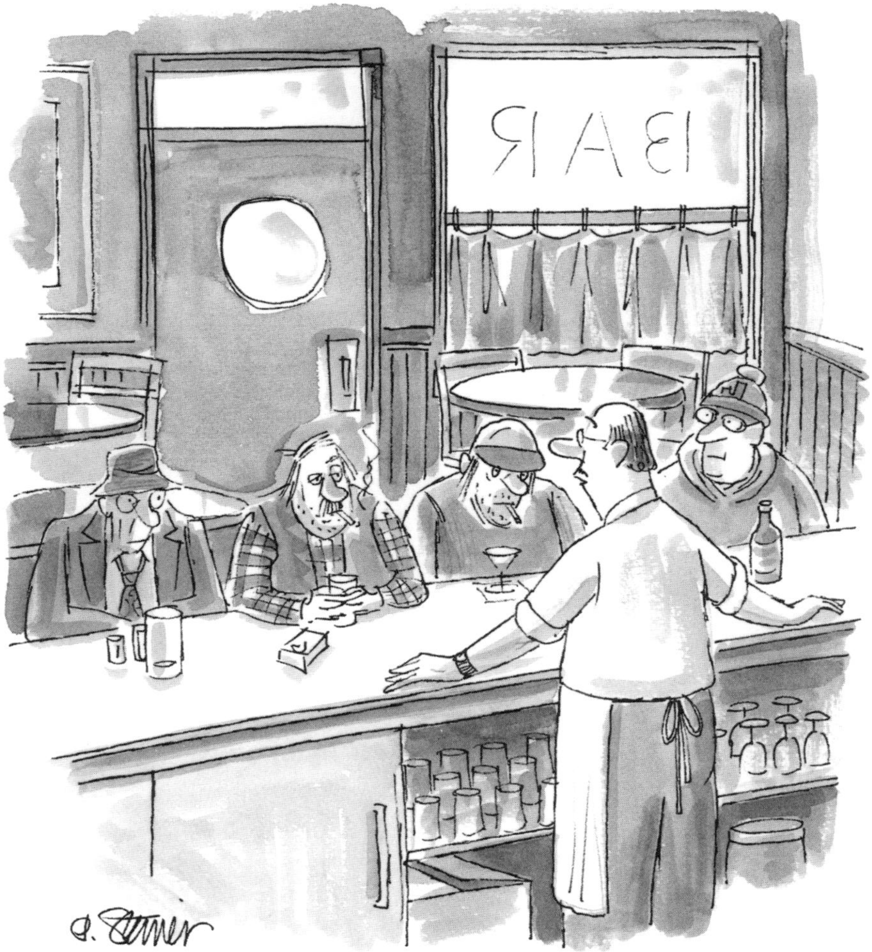
BAR

"What would you boys think if we started selling books?"

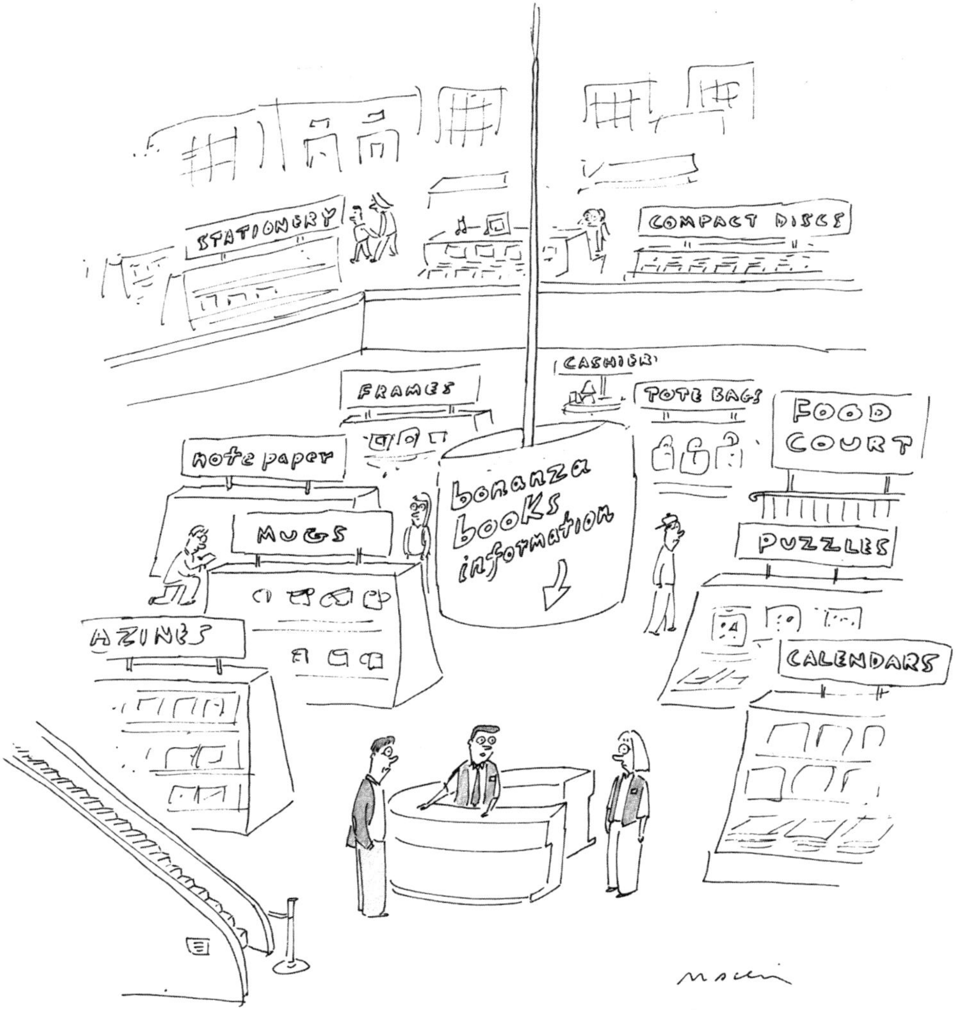
STATIONERY
COMPACT DISCS
CASHIER
FRAMES
TOTE BAGS
FOOD COURT
note paper
MUGS
bonanza books information
PUZZLES
AZINES
CALENDARS

"Mona, would you help this gentleman find a book?"

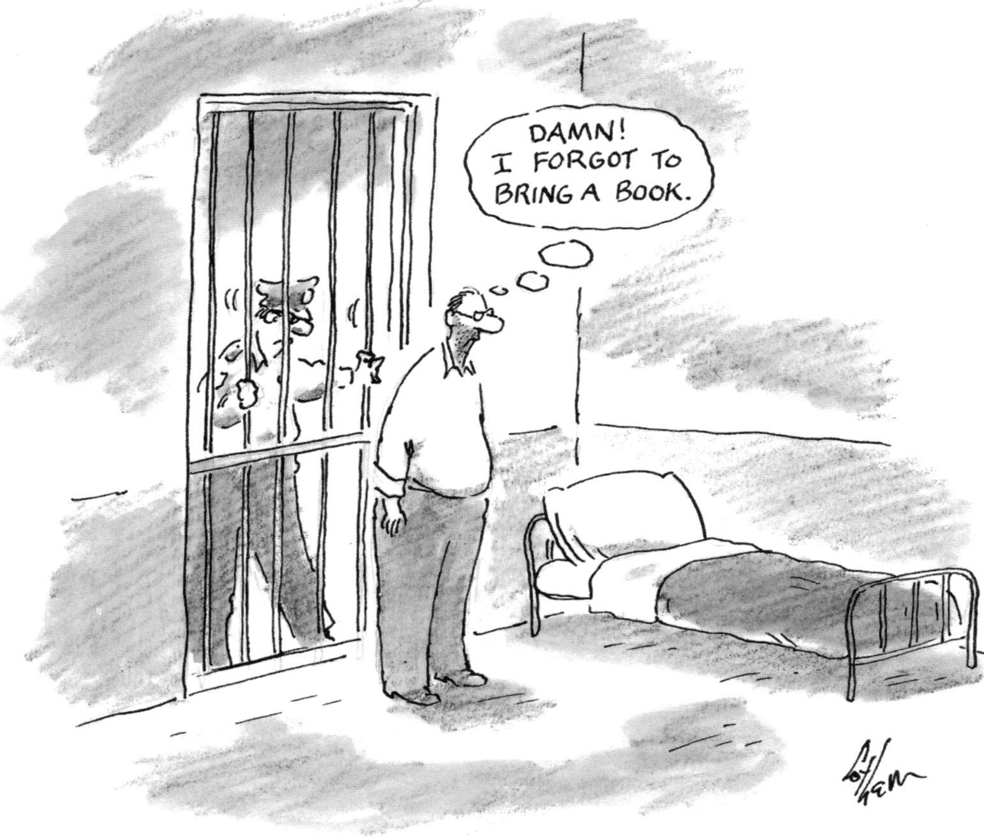
DAMN!
I FORGOT TO
BRING A BOOK.

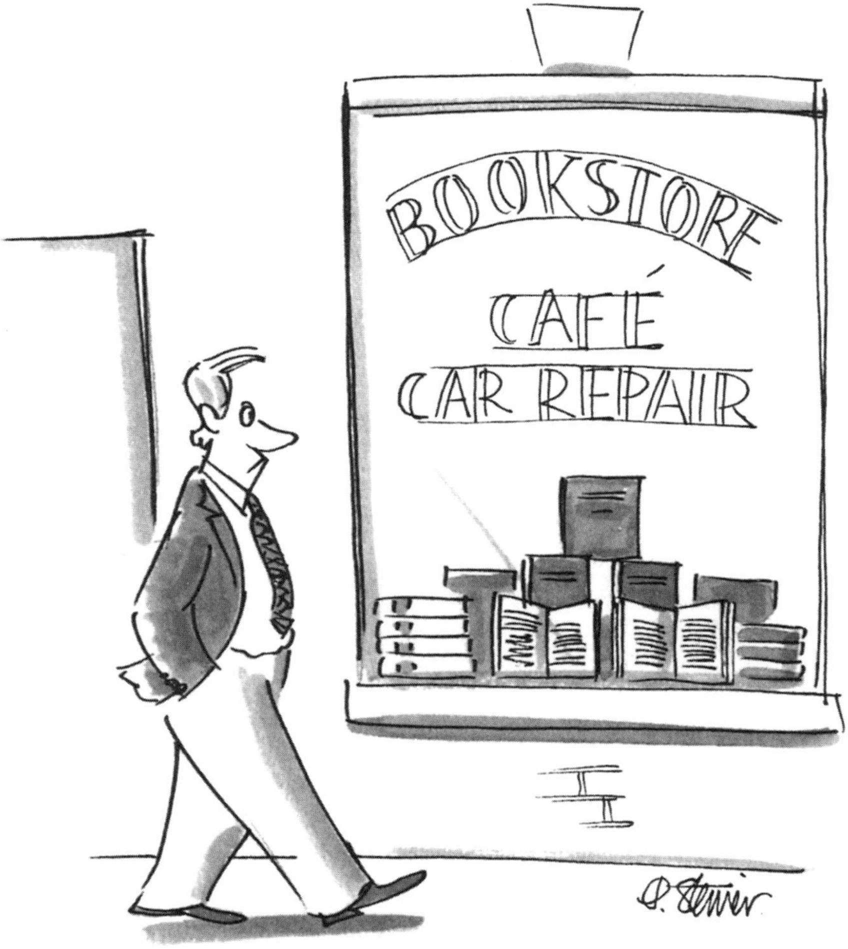
BOOKSTORE
CAFÉ
CAR REPAIR
P. Steiner

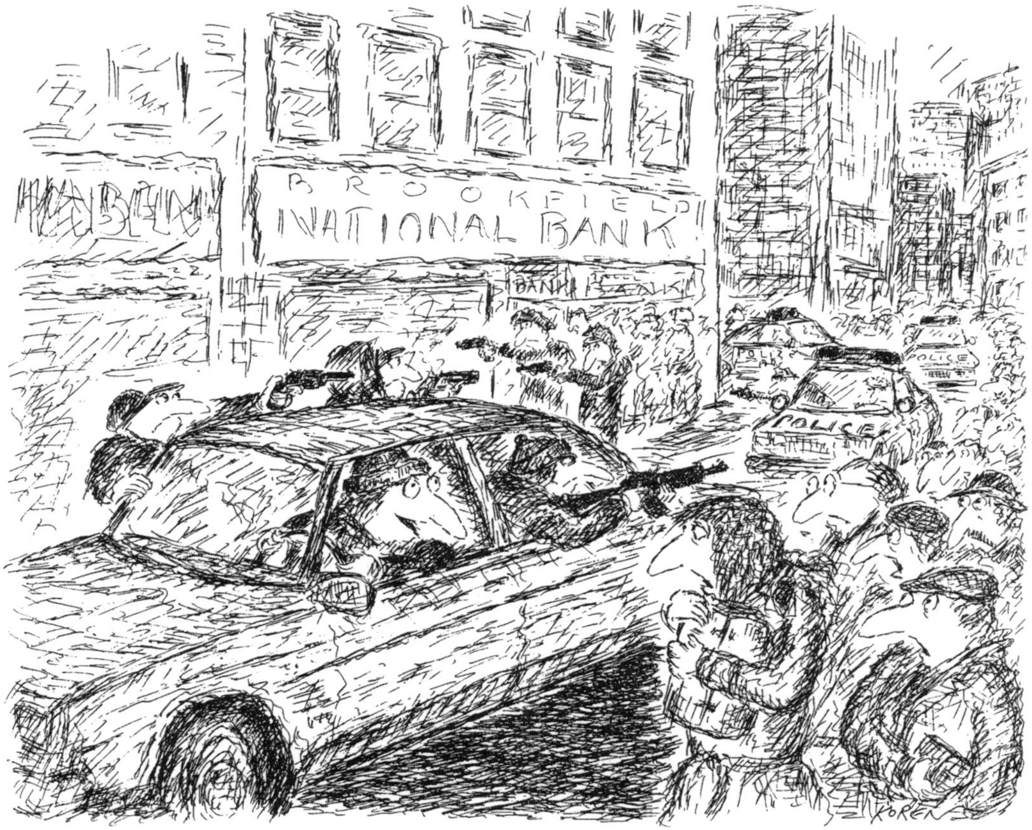
BROOKFIELD
NATIONAL BANK
POLICE
POLICE
POLICE
KOREN

"I'm only doing this to support my writing."

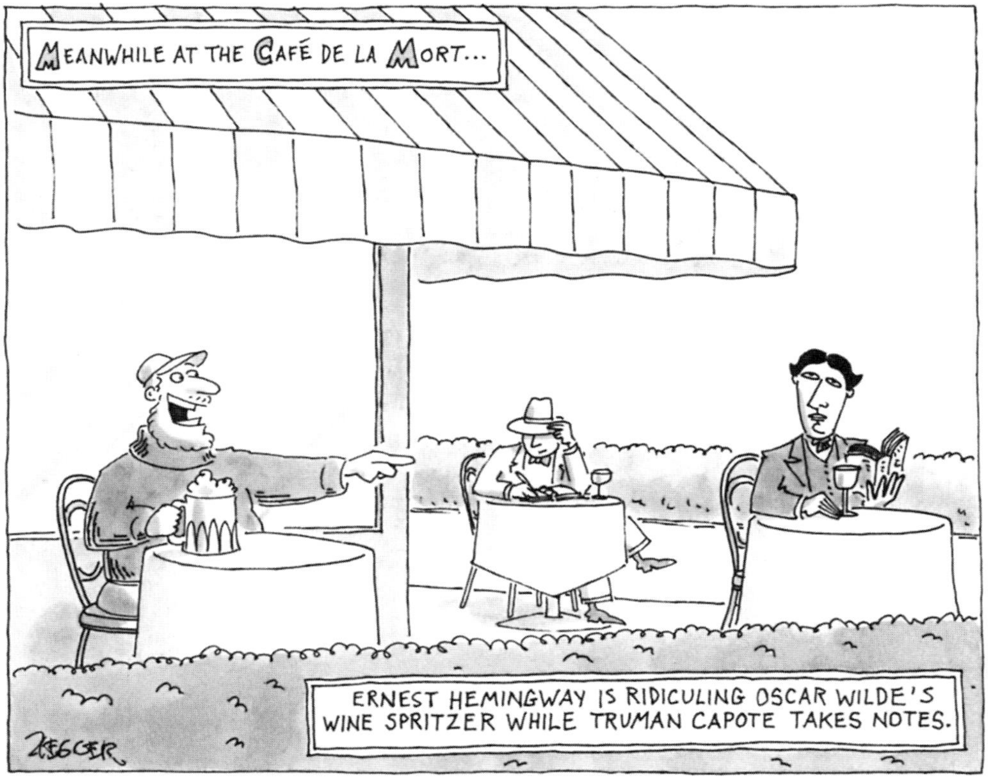
MEANWHILE AT THE CAFÉ DE LA MORT...
ERNEST HEMINGWAY IS RIDICULING OSCAR WILDE'S WINE SPRITZER WHILE TRUMAN CAPOTE TAKES NOTES.

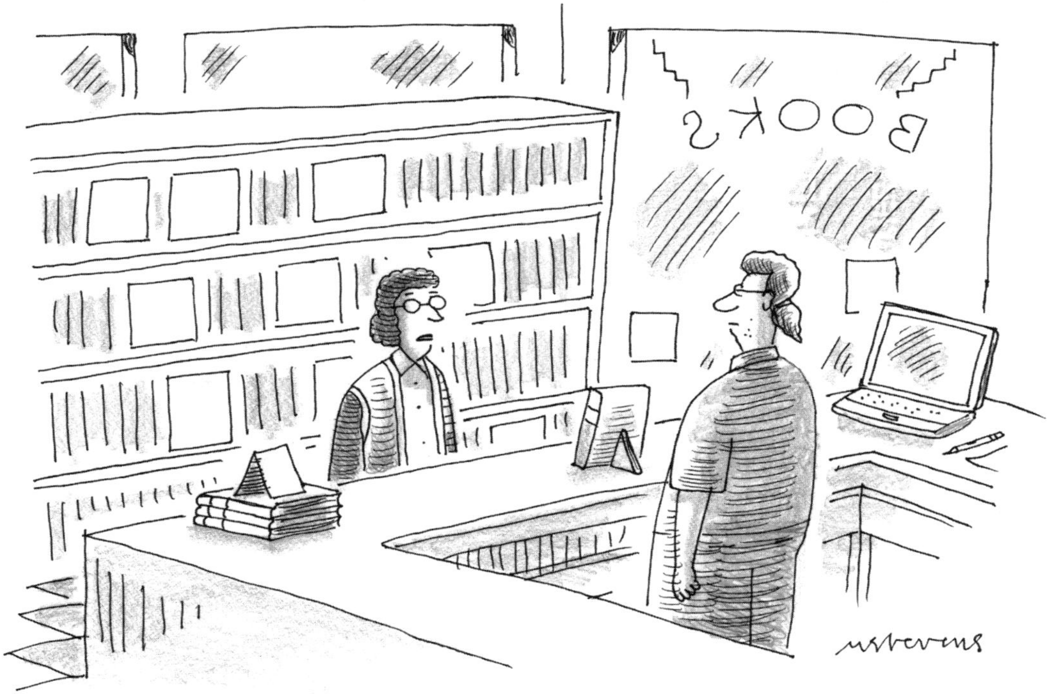
BOOKS
mstevens

"I'm looking for a book by T. What's-His-Face Boyle."

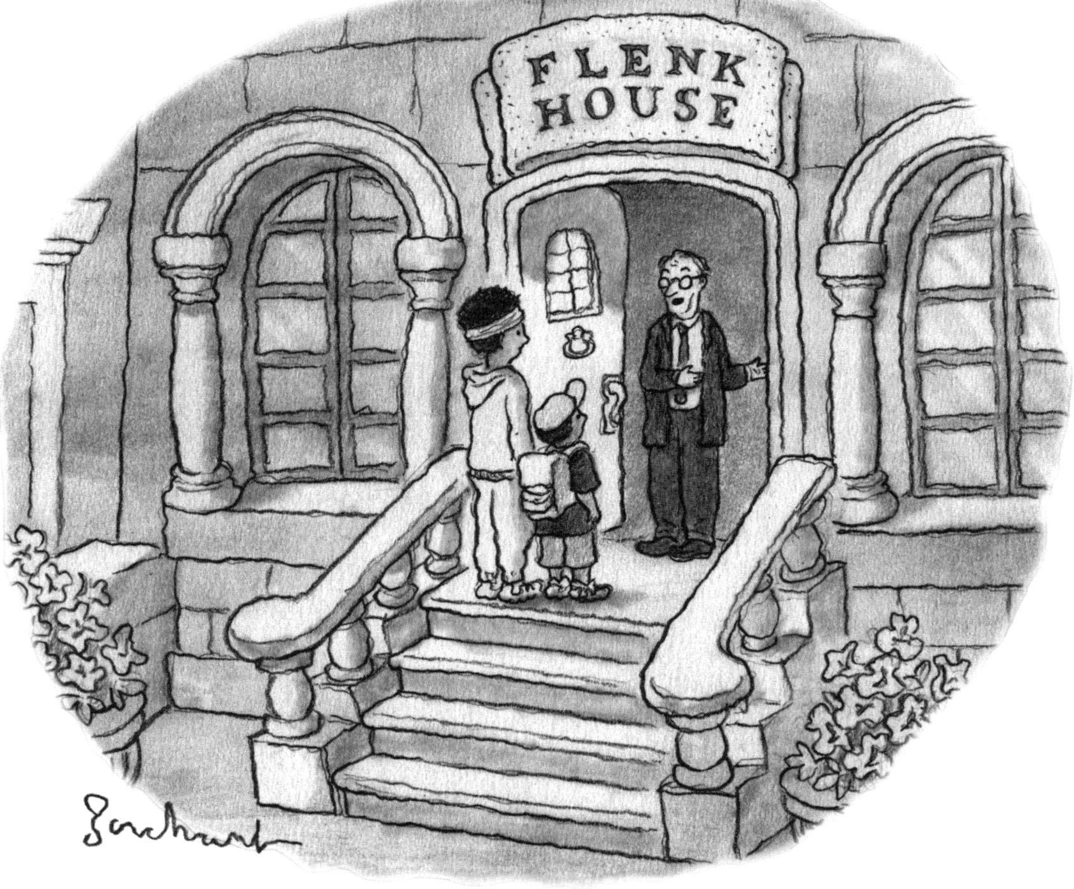
FLENK
HOUSE

"The restroom is through the bookstore, but be warned—it could be the first step on a lifelong odyssey into the works of Otto Eugeus Flenk."

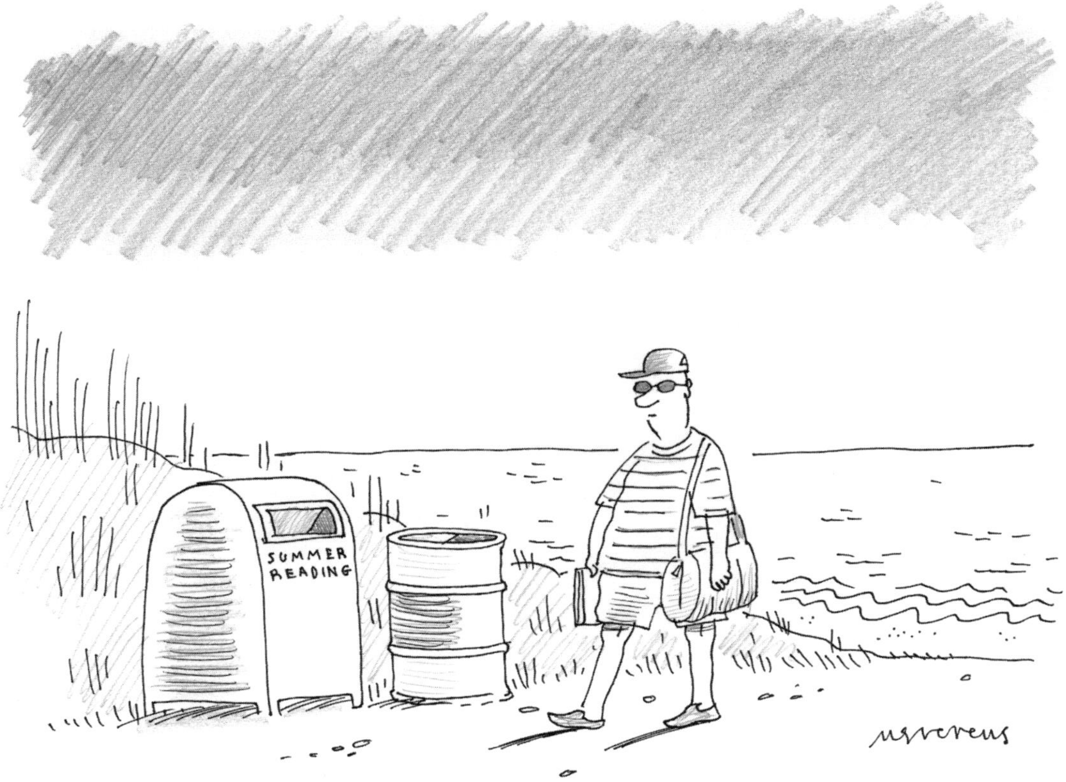
SUMMER
READING

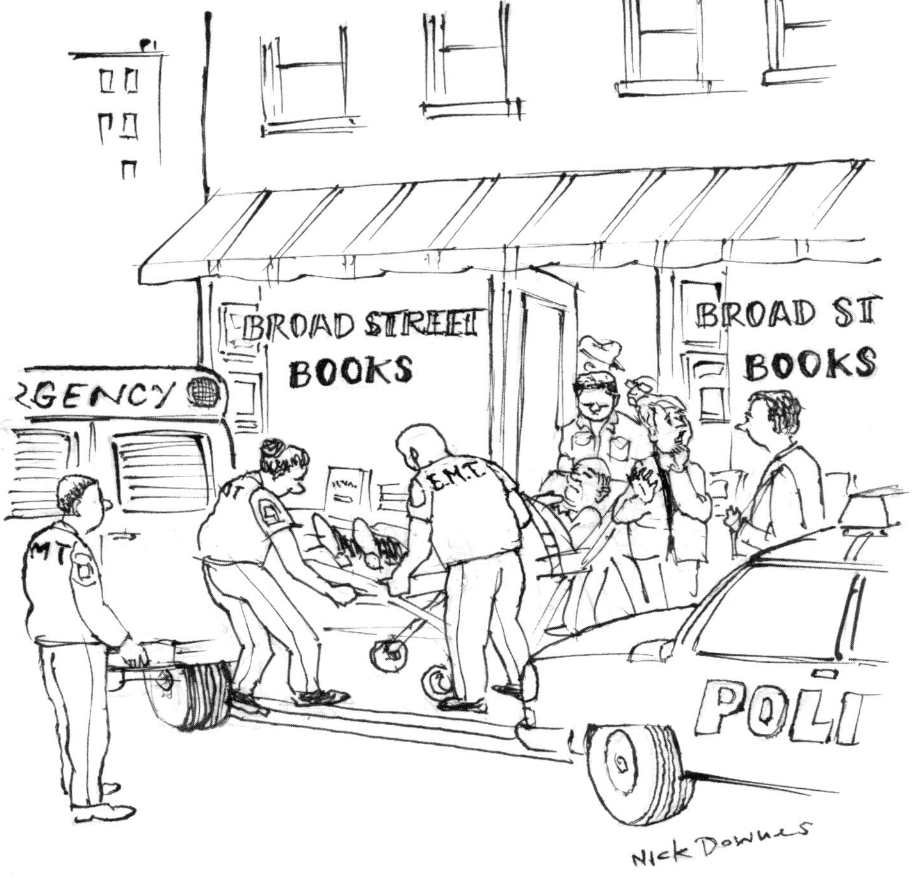
BROAD STREET
BOOKS
BROAD ST
BOOKS
RGENCY
E.M.T.
MT
POLI
Nick Downes

"It was horrible—the Joyce Carol Oates section caved in on him!"

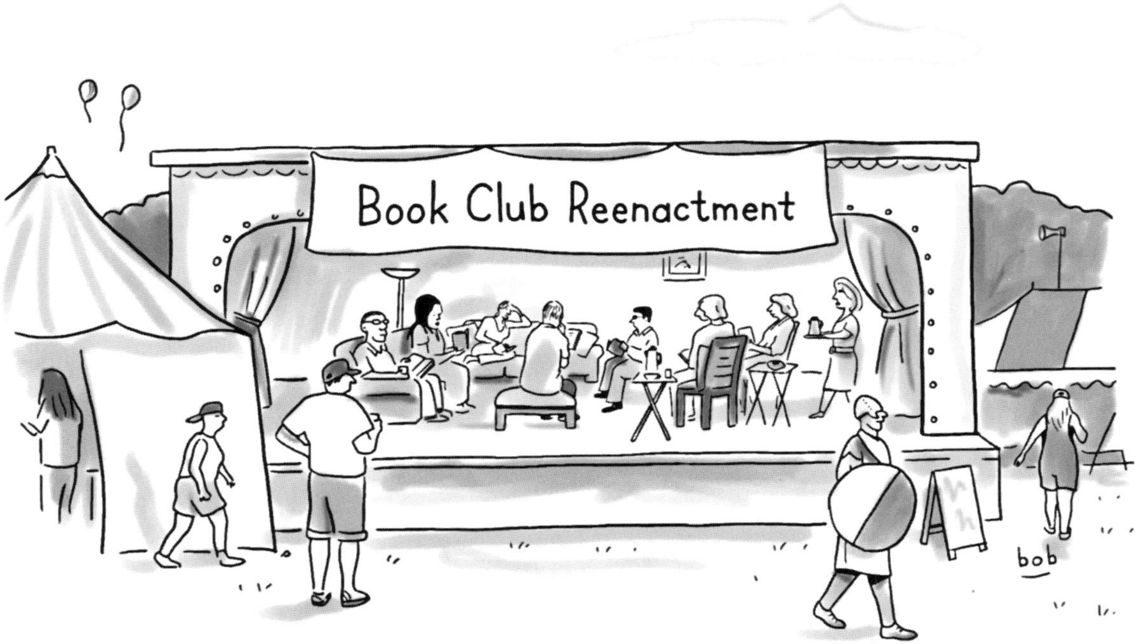
Book Club Reenactment
bob

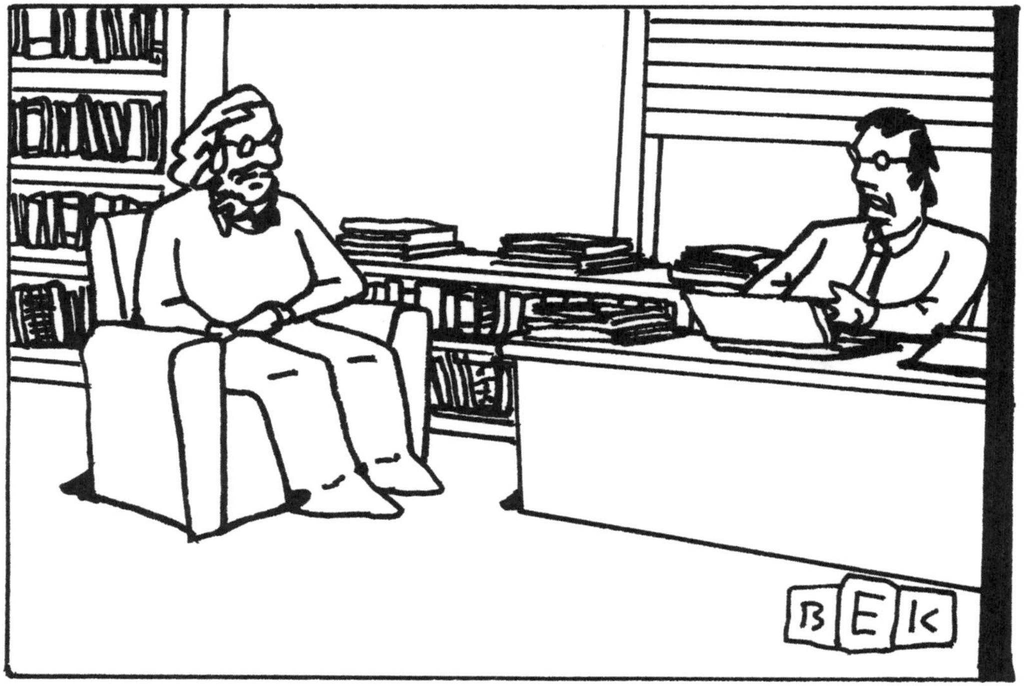
BEK

"I'm sorry—you tapped into something no one cares about."

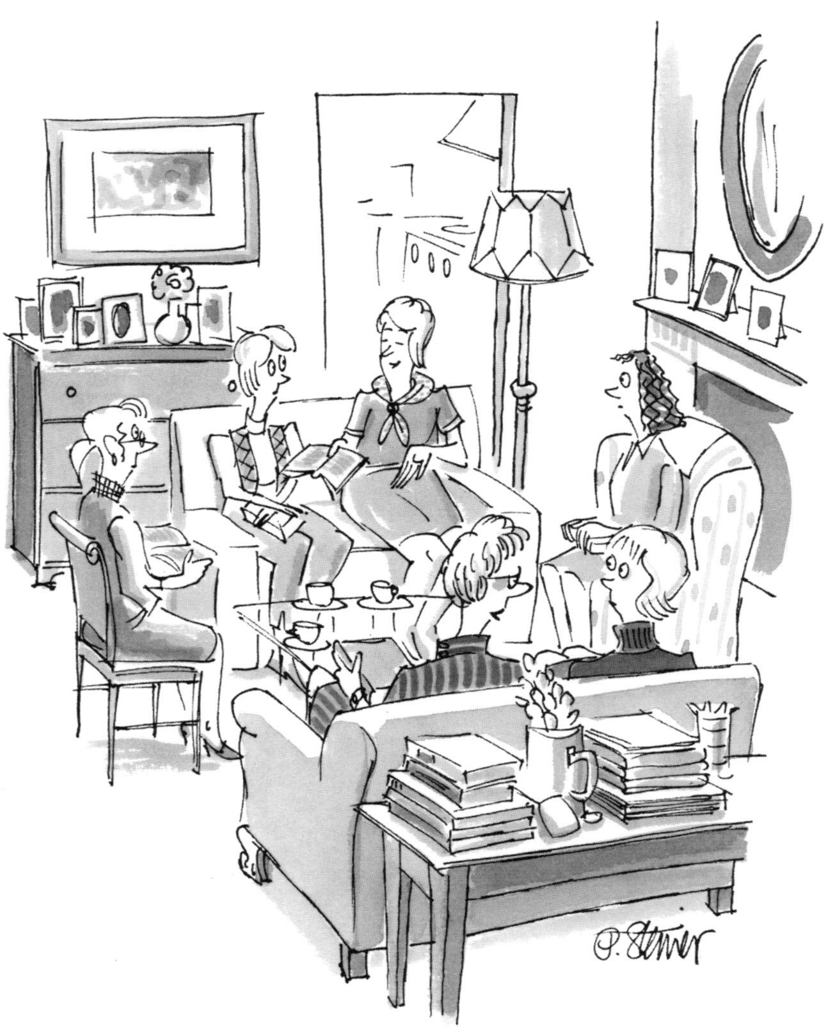
P. Steiner

"She's promiscuous. She's in five book groups."

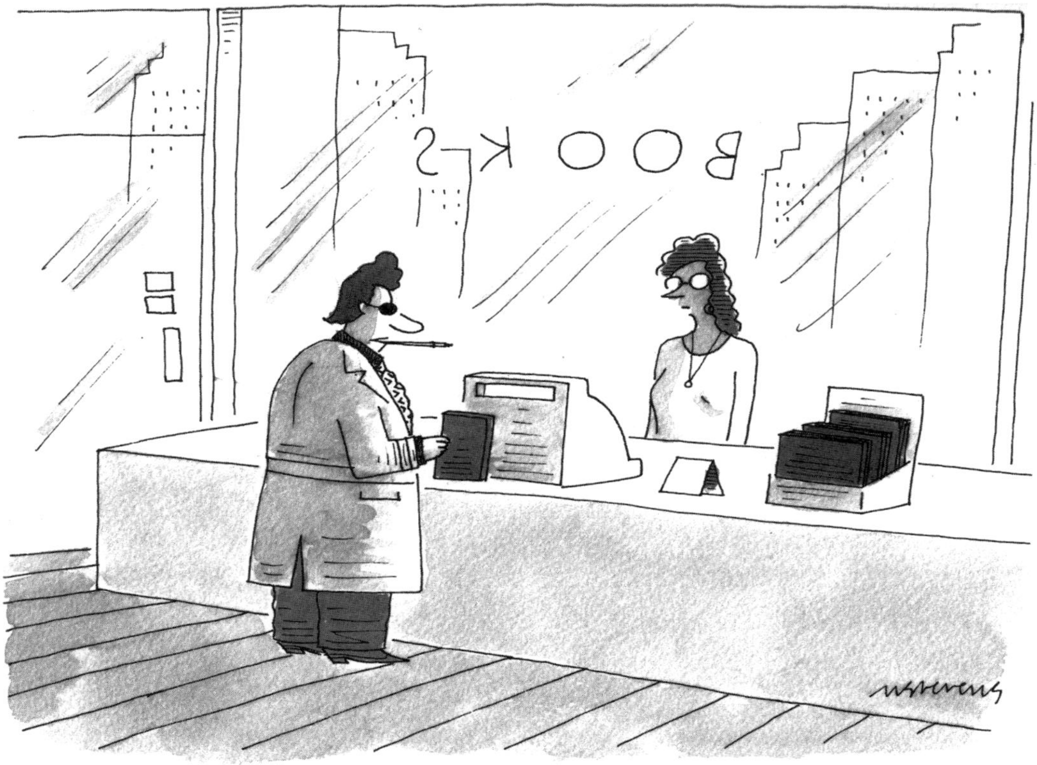
BOOKS

"I'd like to buy this book and also the movie rights."

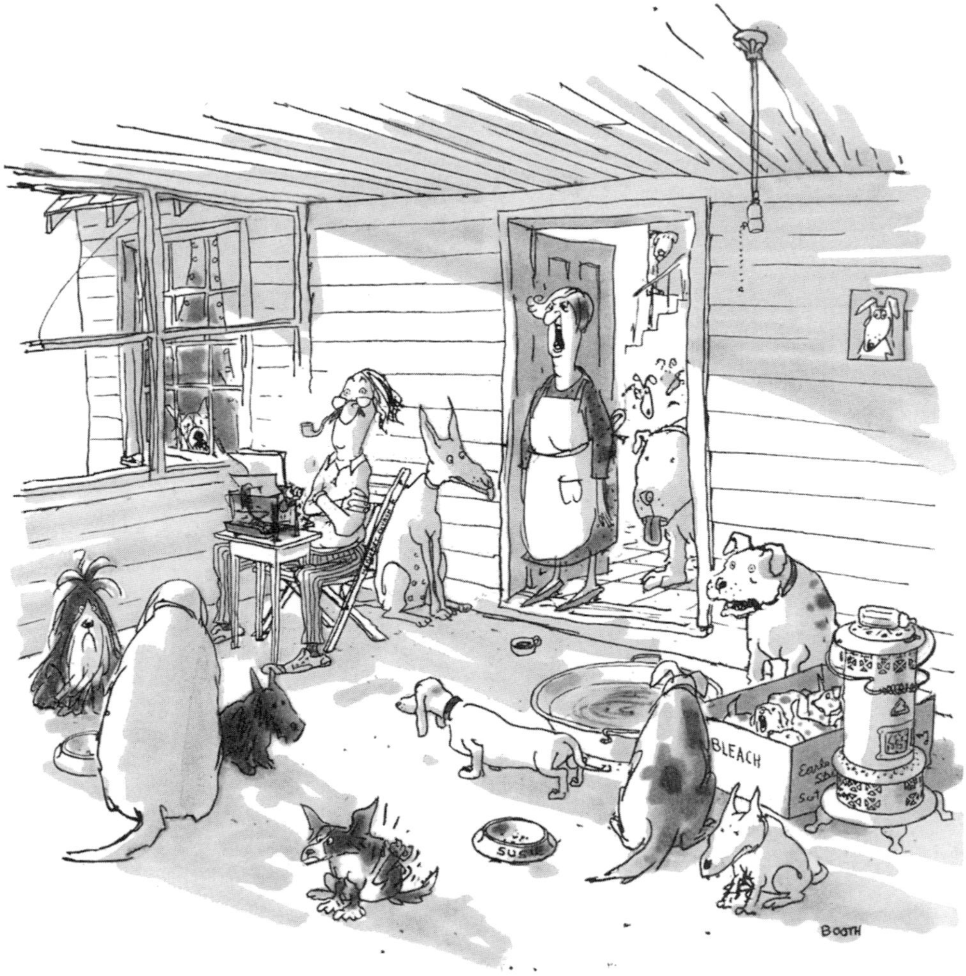
BLEACH
BOOTH

"Write about dogs!"

"Our bookstore rat."

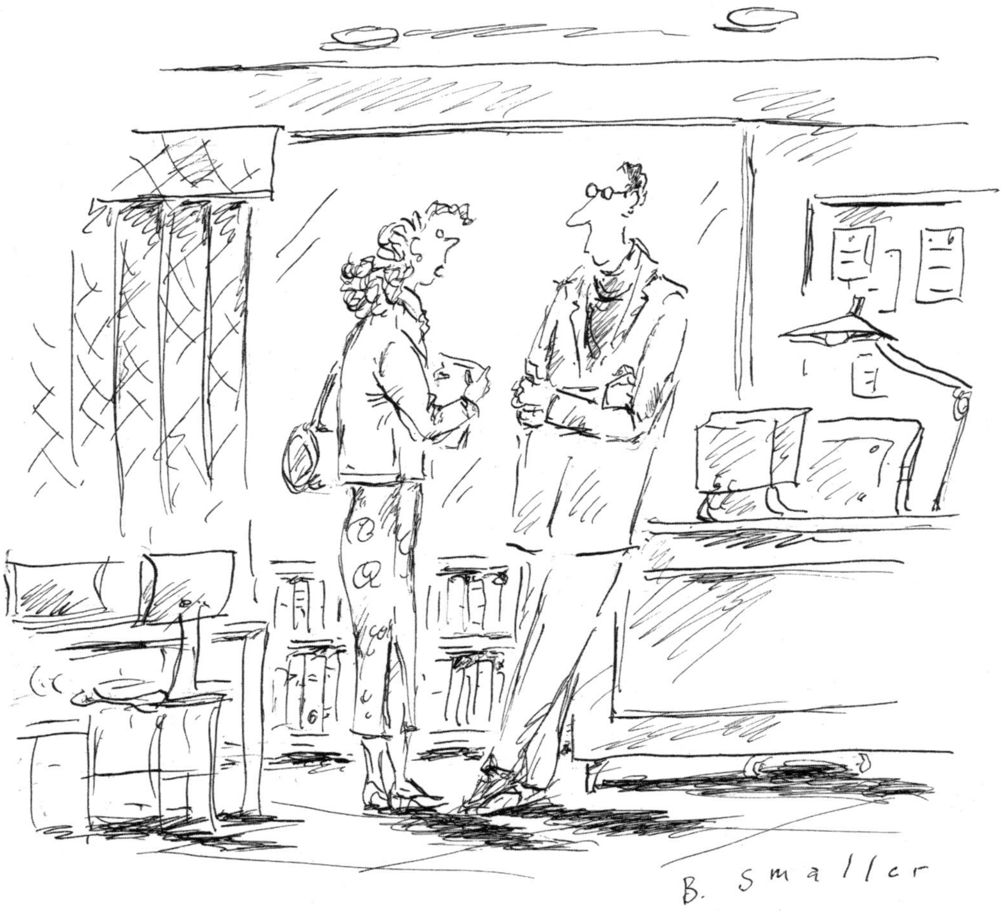
B. Smaller

"I want to write what I know, but all I know is writing workshops."

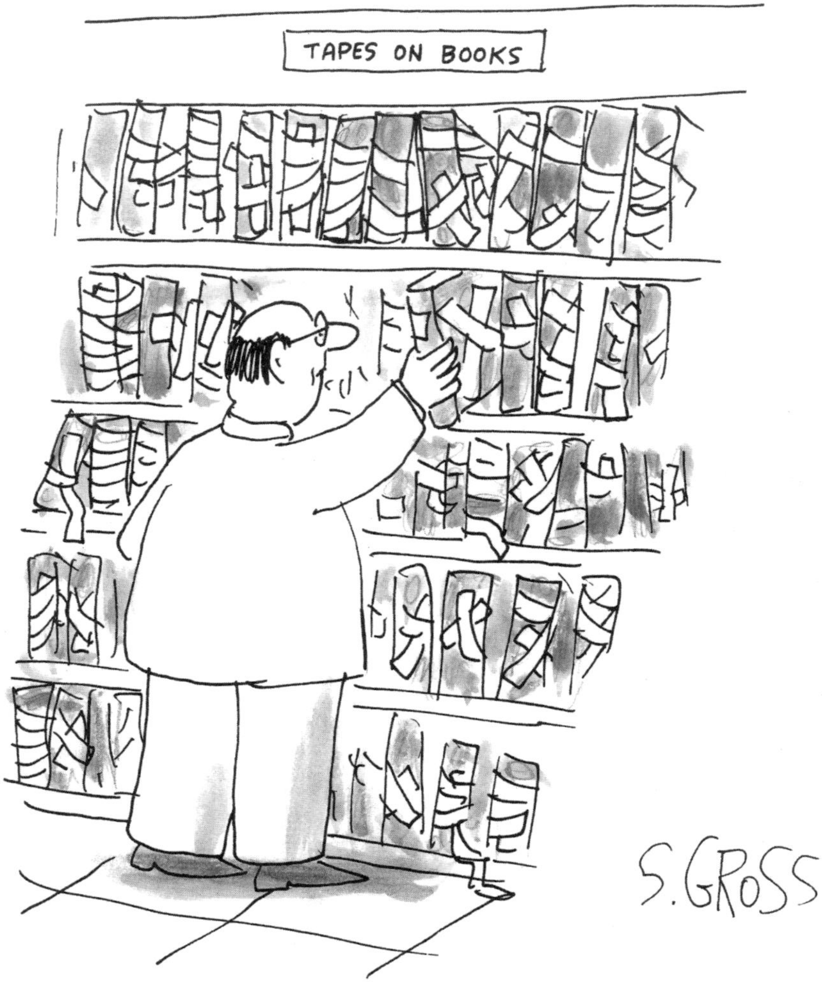
TAPES ON BOOKS
S. GROSS

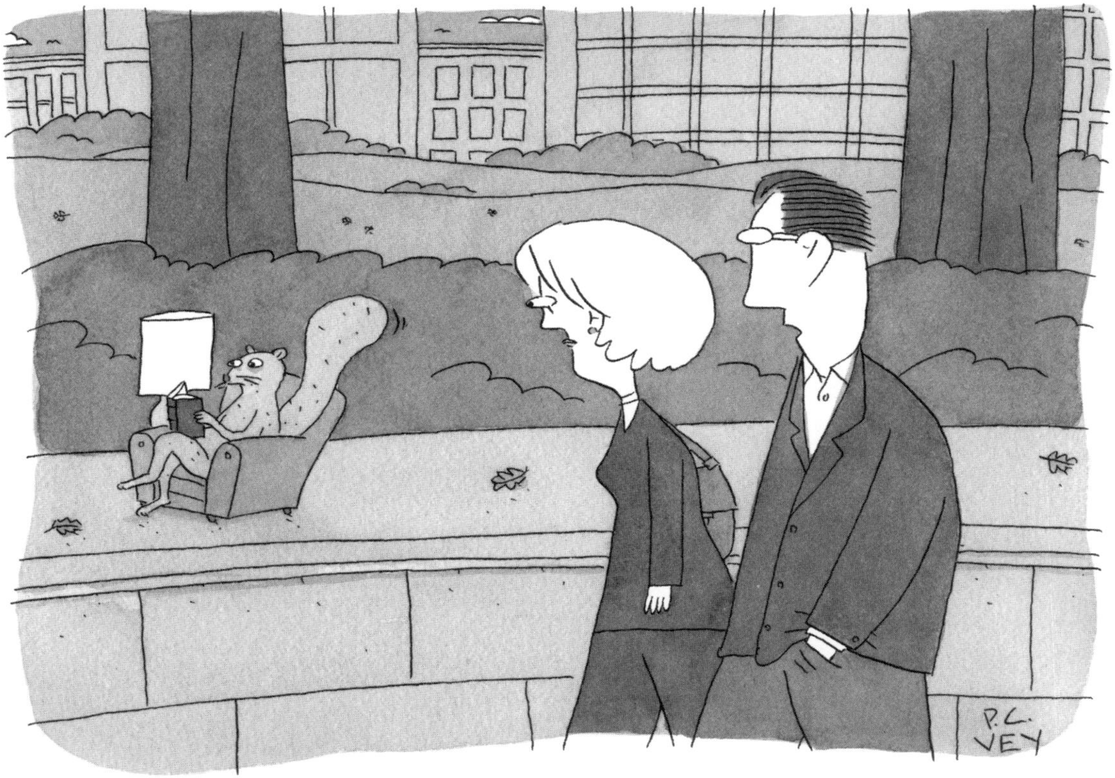
P.C. VEY

"It's unusual to see them reading this time of year."

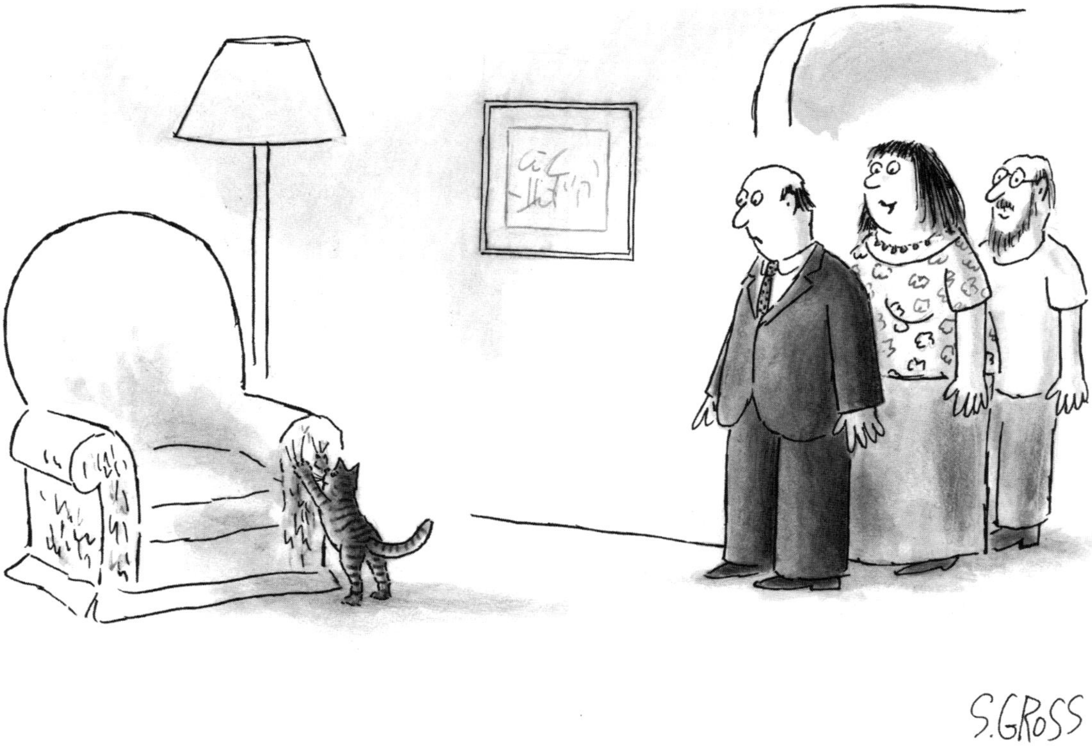
S.GROSS

"We believe that in a former life she was an editor."

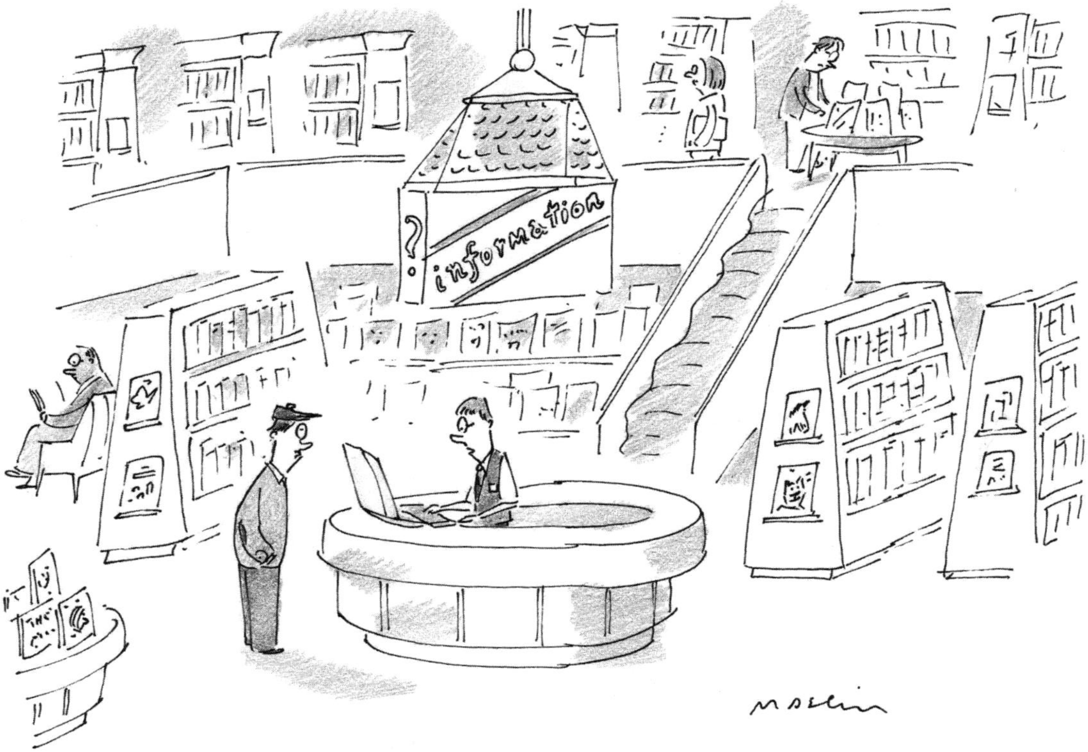
information

"'The Men's Room' isn't coming up on my computer. Do you have the name of the author or the publisher?"

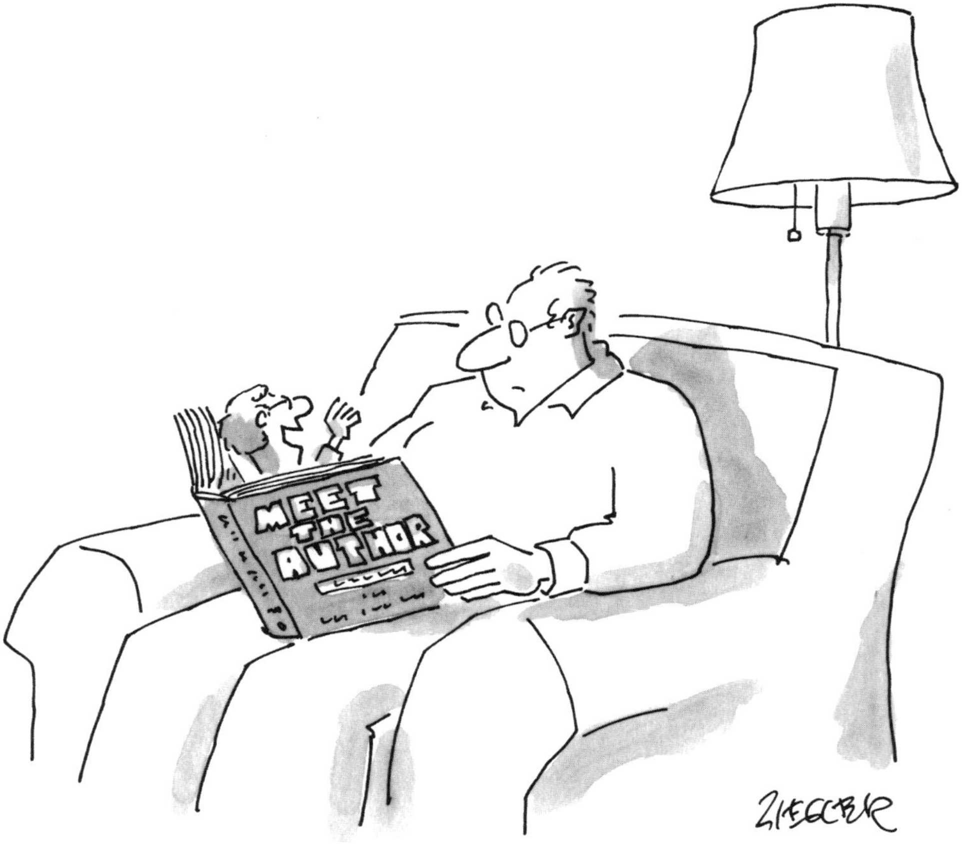
MEET THE AUTHOR

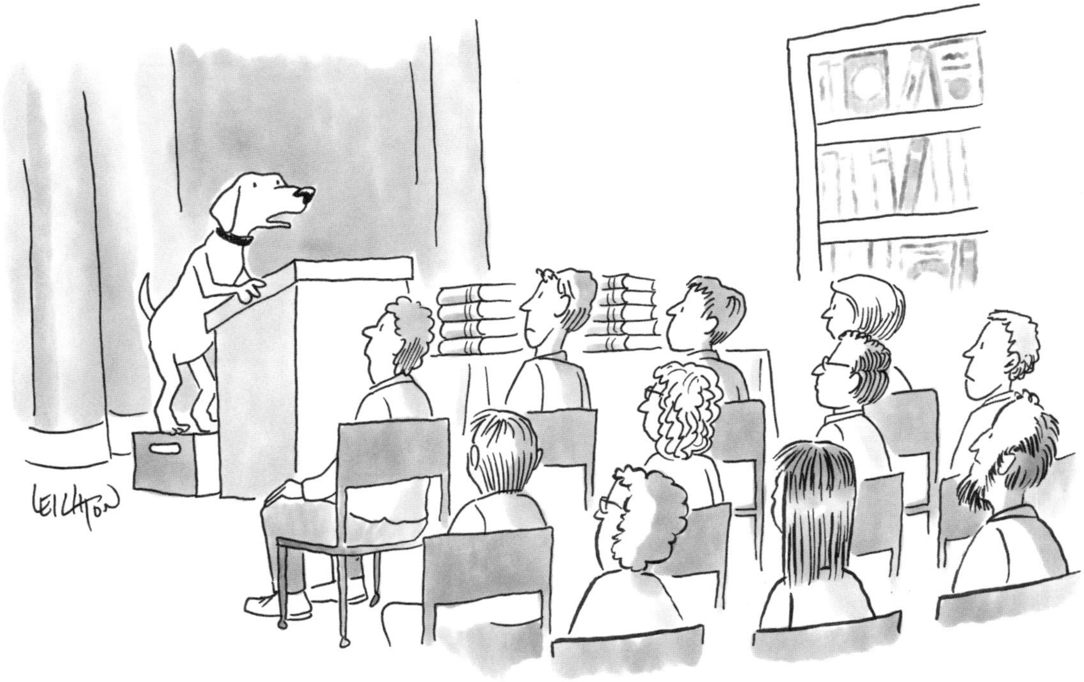
LEIGHTON

“Mostly, I wanted to clear up the misperception that I was merely his companion.”

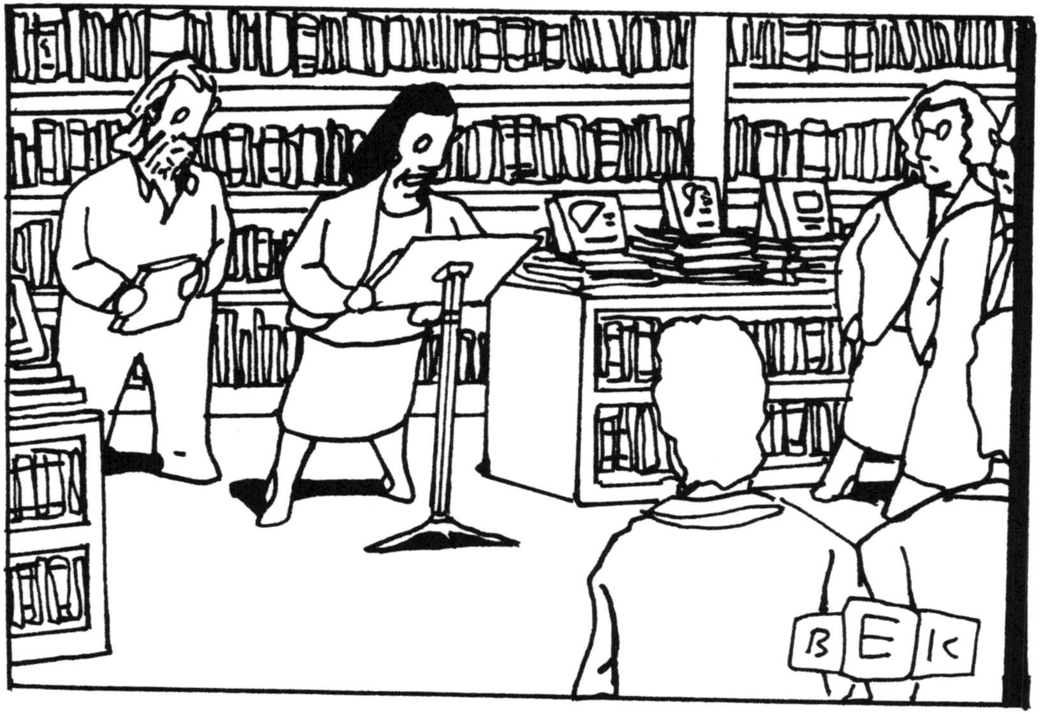
BEK

"There's an informal Q and A, and then, afterward, the author's sad flirting with some fan."

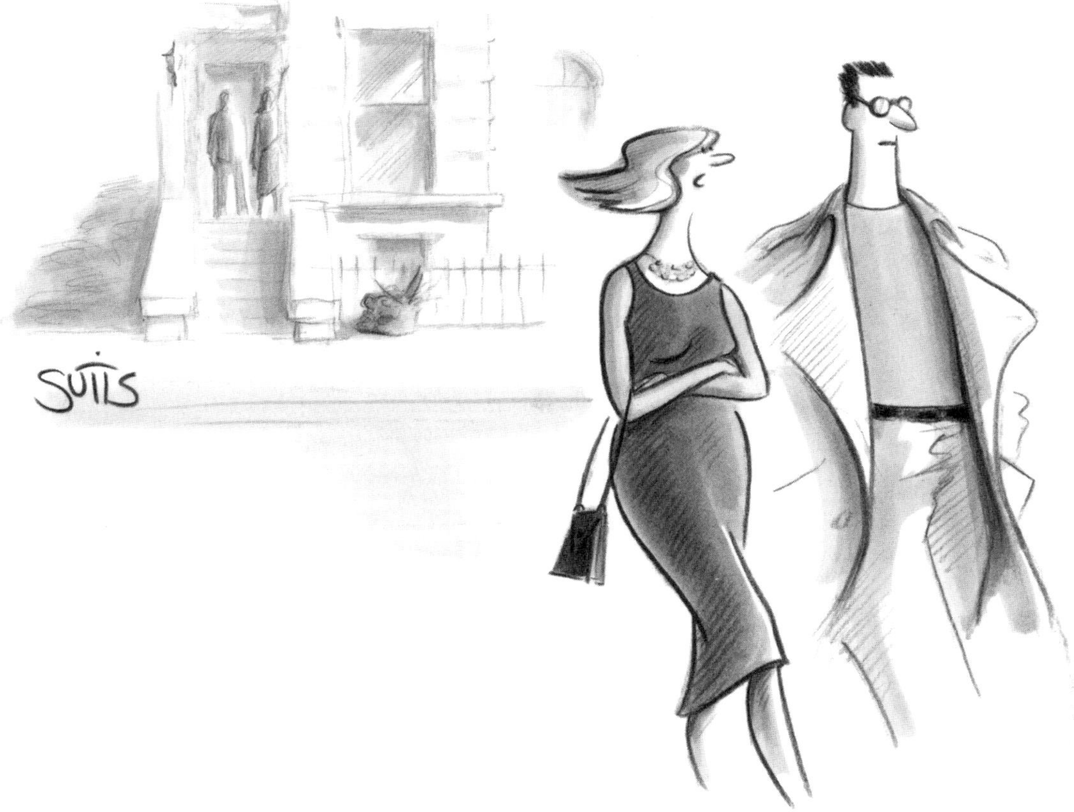
SUTILS

"Their bookshelves look more convincingly read from than ours."

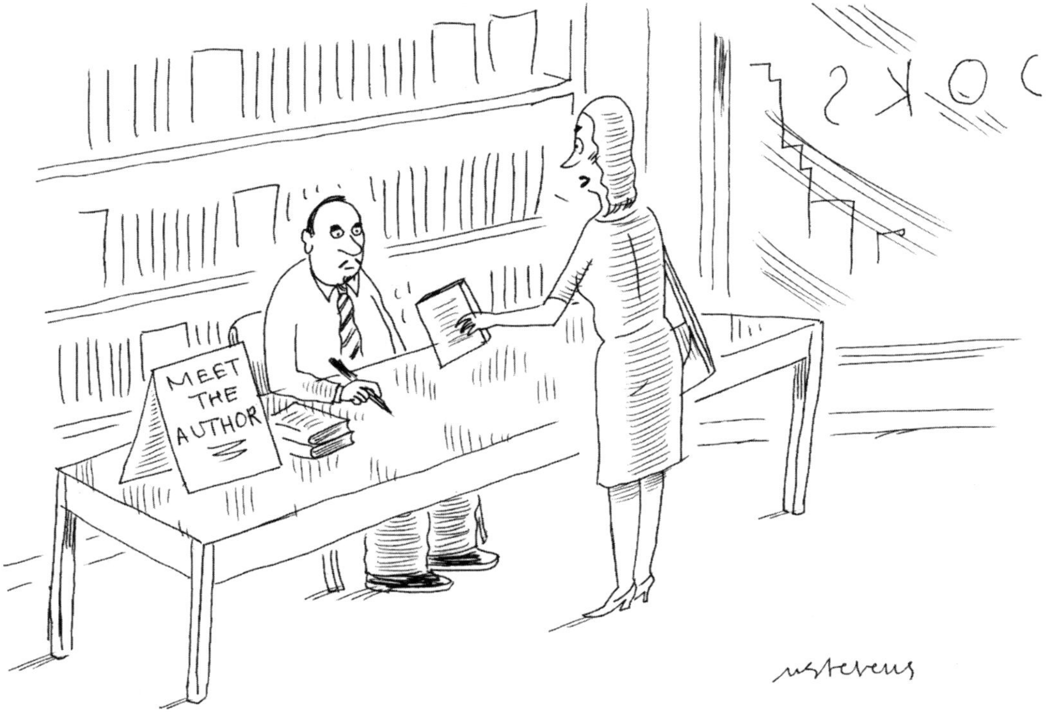
MEET
THE
AUTHOR

"I don't want you to sign it. I want my money back."

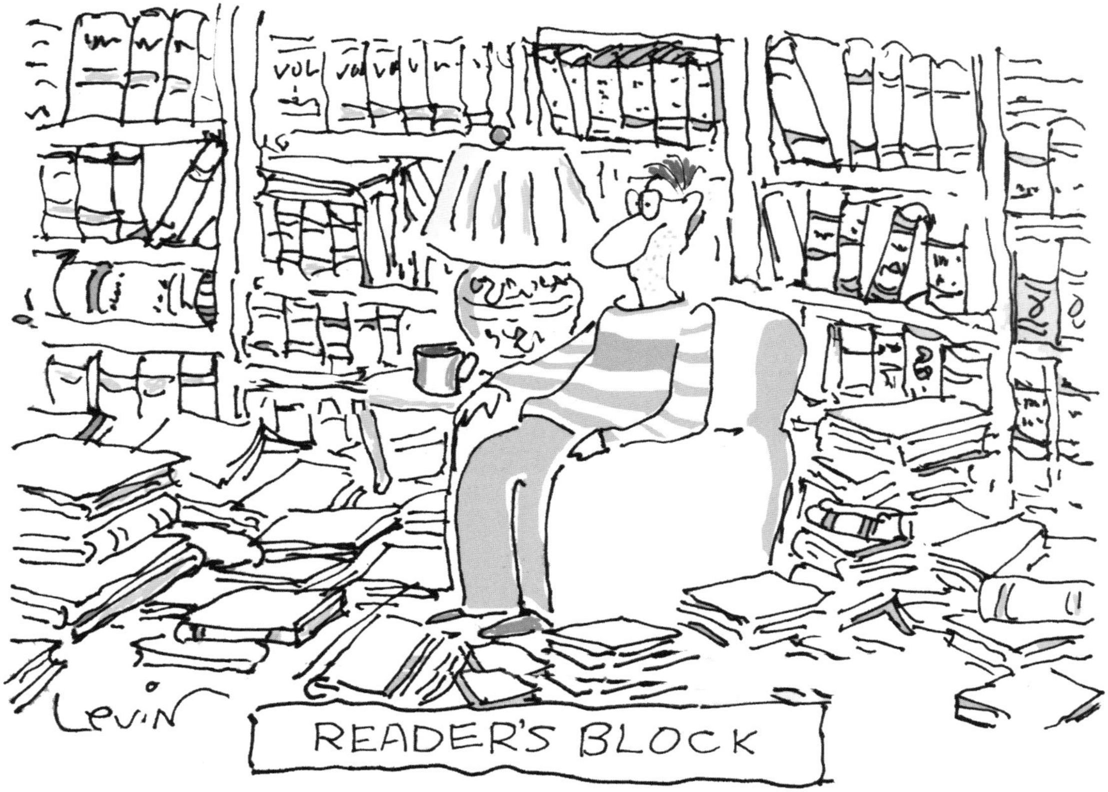
VOL
LEVIN
READER'S BLOCK

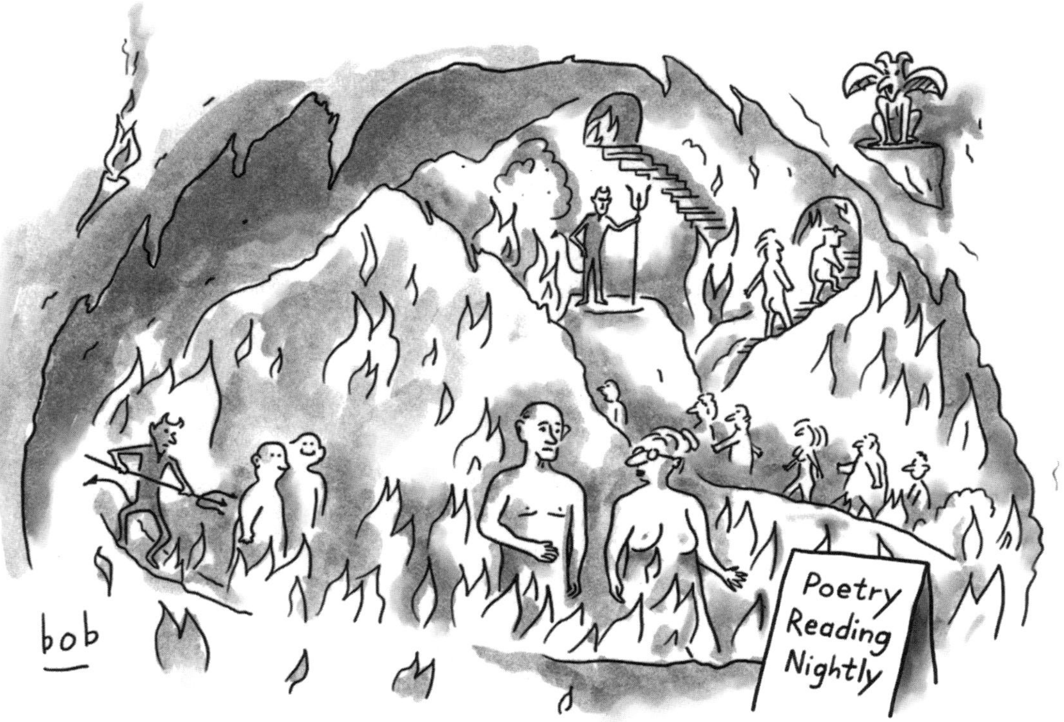
bob
Poetry Reading Nightly

"Bad news—looks like we've got a bestseller on our hands."

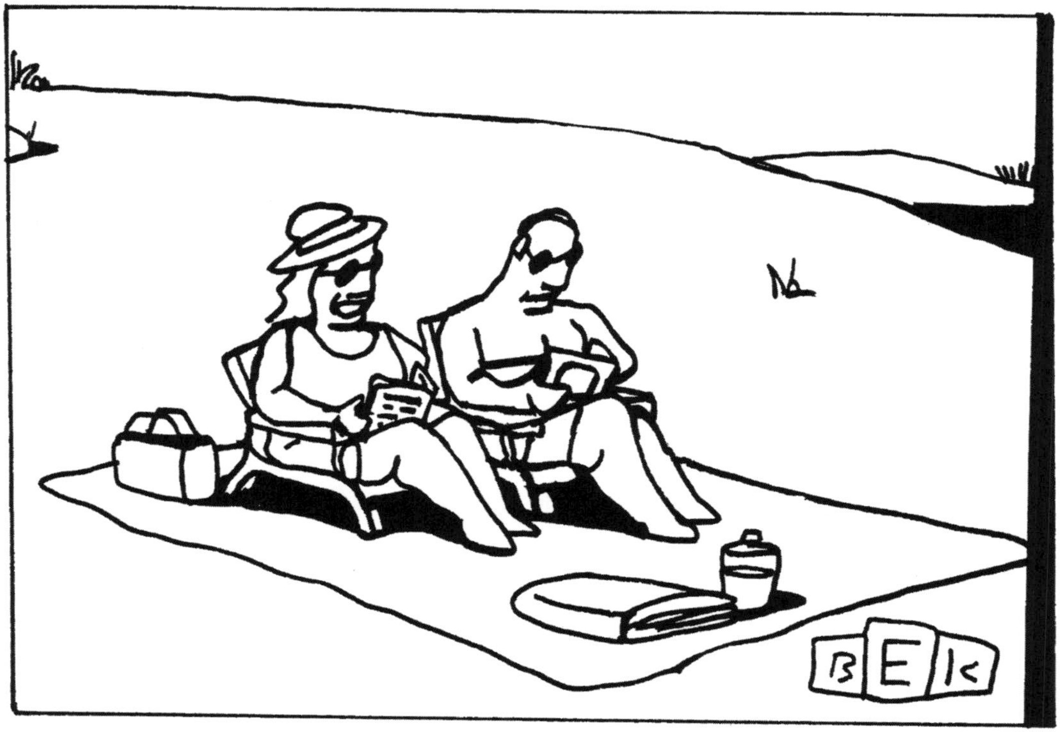
BEK

"I love my unreliable narrator. You?"

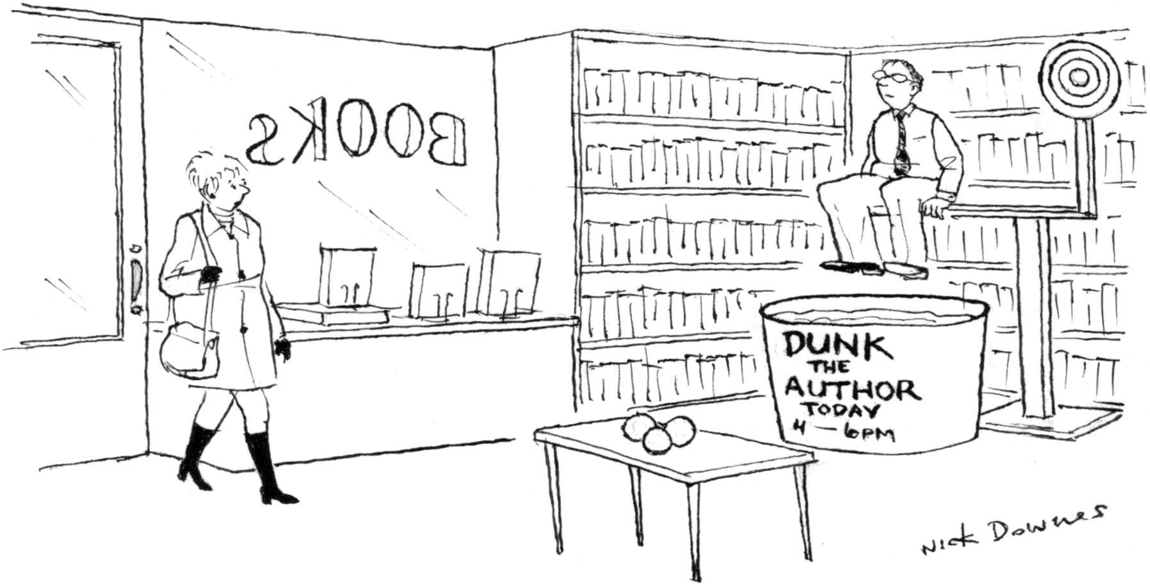
BOOKS
DUNK THE AUTHOR TODAY 4—6PM
Nick Downes

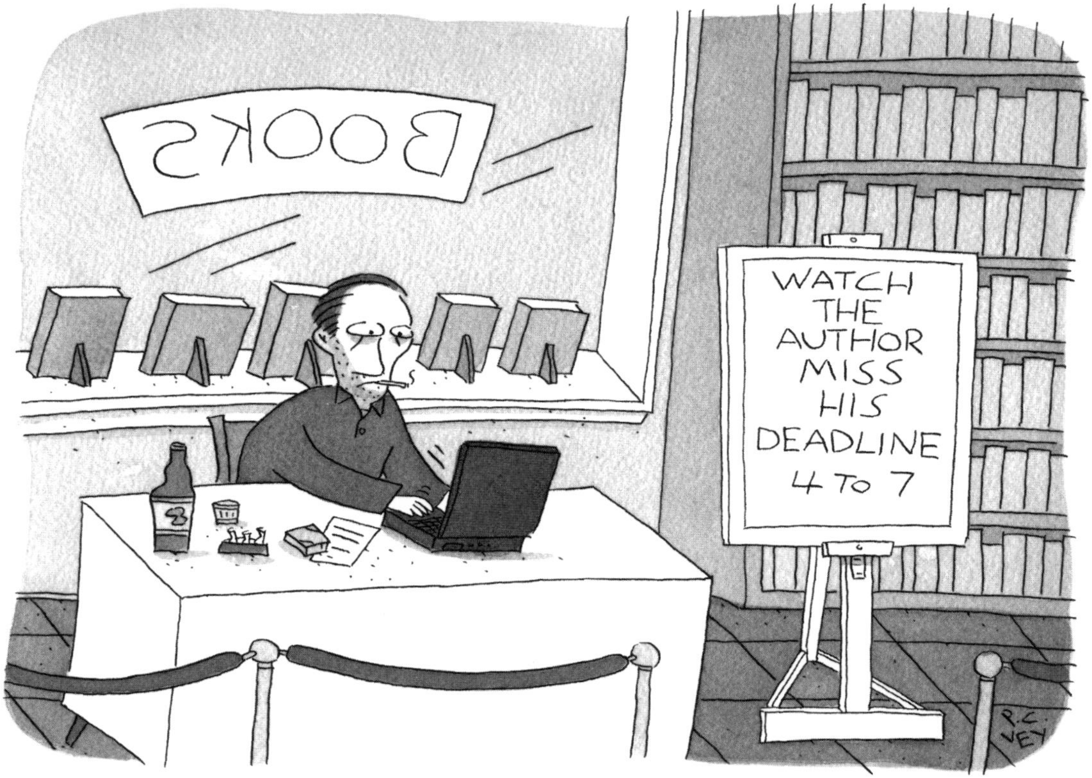
BOOKS
WATCH THE AUTHOR MISS HIS DEADLINE
4 TO 7
P.C. VEY

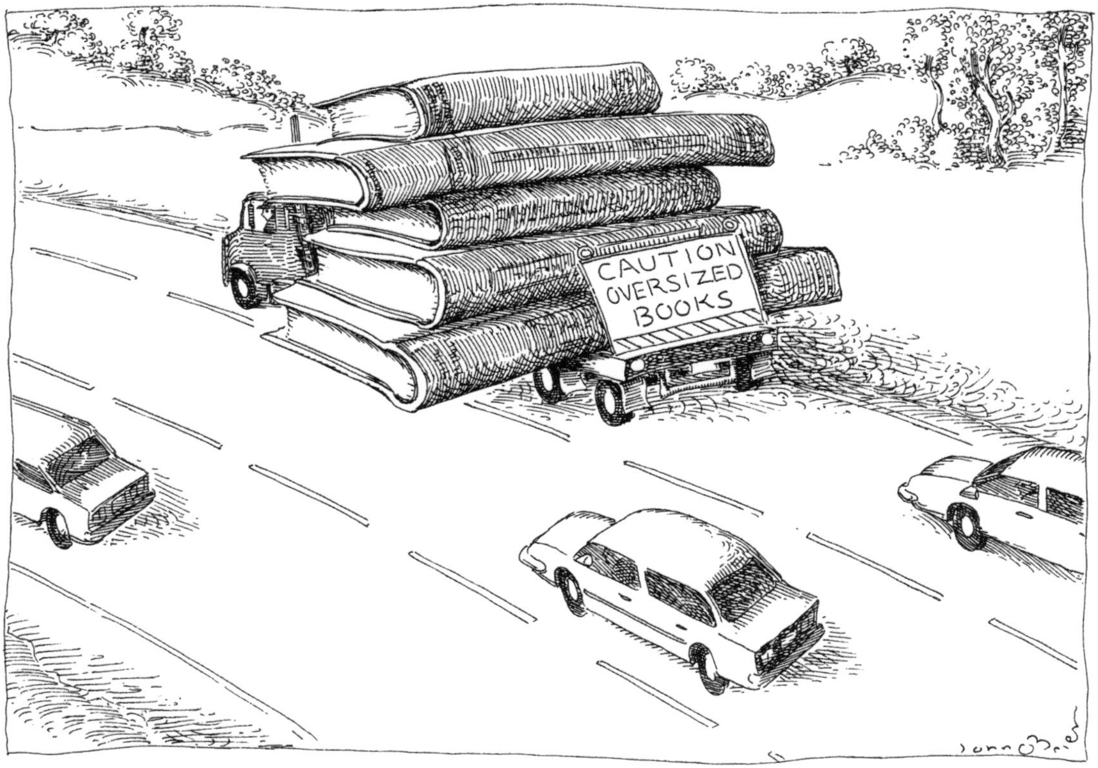
CAUTION
OVERSIZED
BOOKS

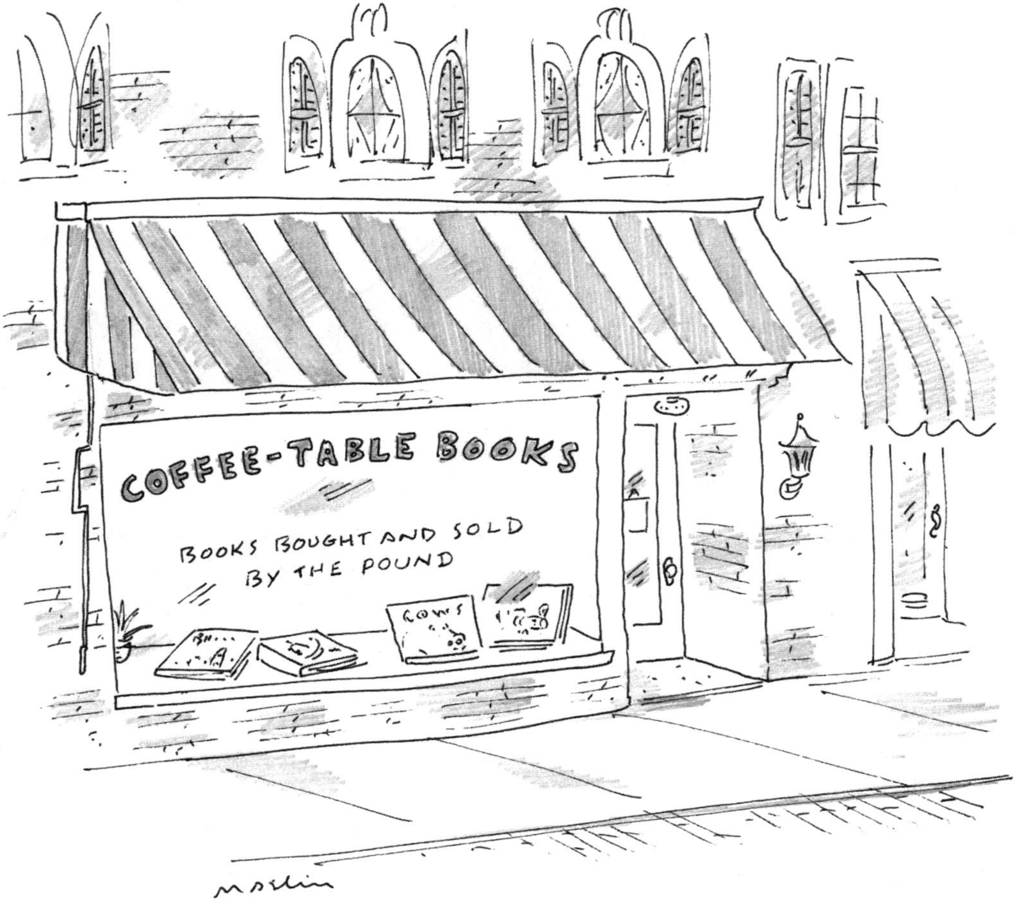
COFFEE-TABLE BOOKS
BOOKS BOUGHT AND SOLD BY THE POUND
COWS

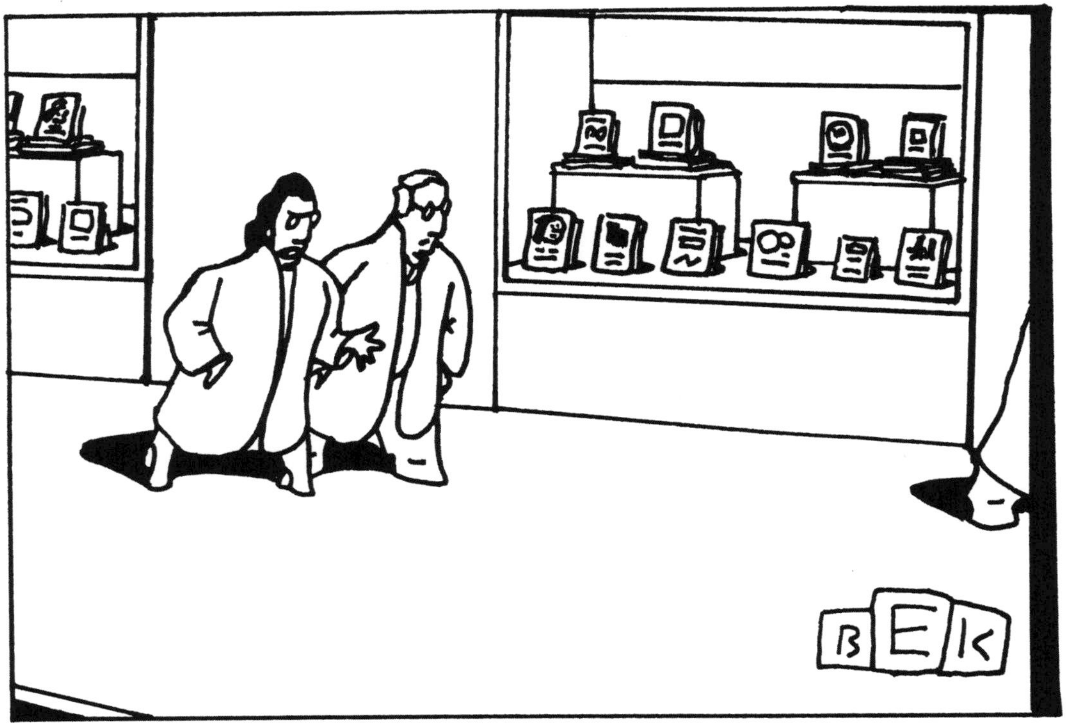
BEK

"Now I have to start pretending I like graphic novels too?"

"Oprah hates beef, but loves to read books, whereas I'm just the opposite."

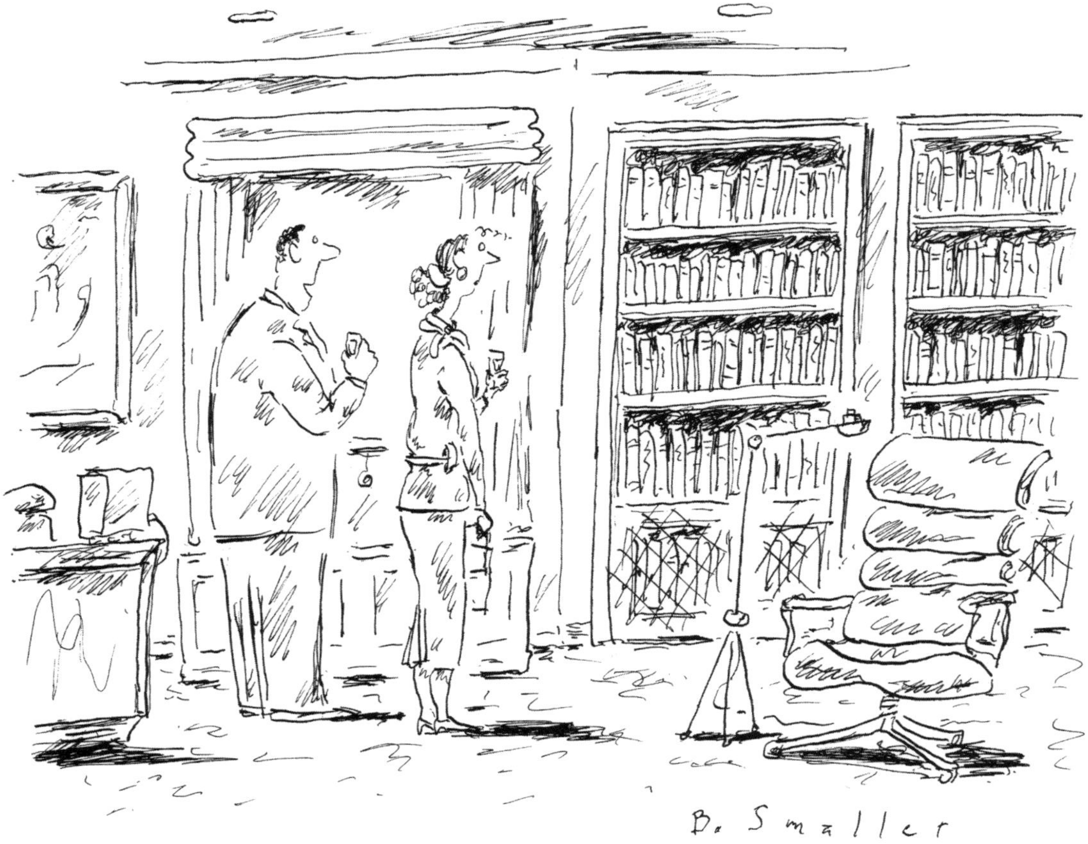
B. Smaller

“Those are the books I never had a chance to finish,
and those are the books I never had a chance to start.”

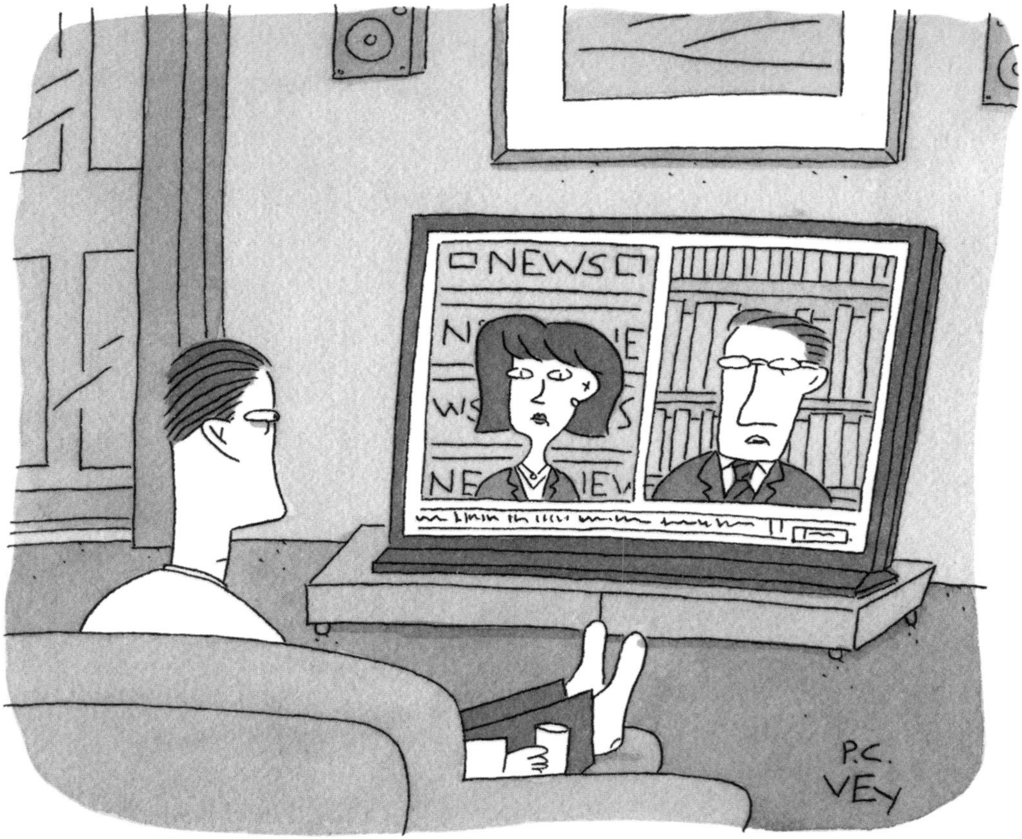
NEWS
P.C.
VEY

"Ann…you can see by the number of books I have behind me that I know what I'm talking about."

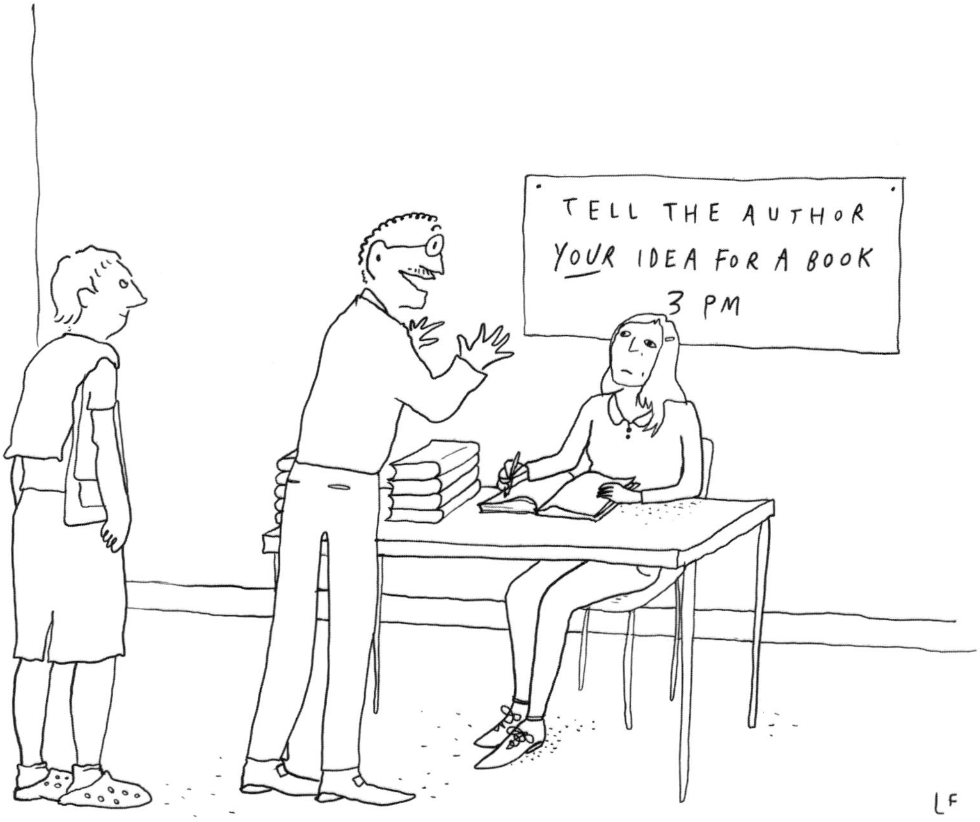
TELL THE AUTHOR
YOUR IDEA FOR A BOOK
3 PM
LF

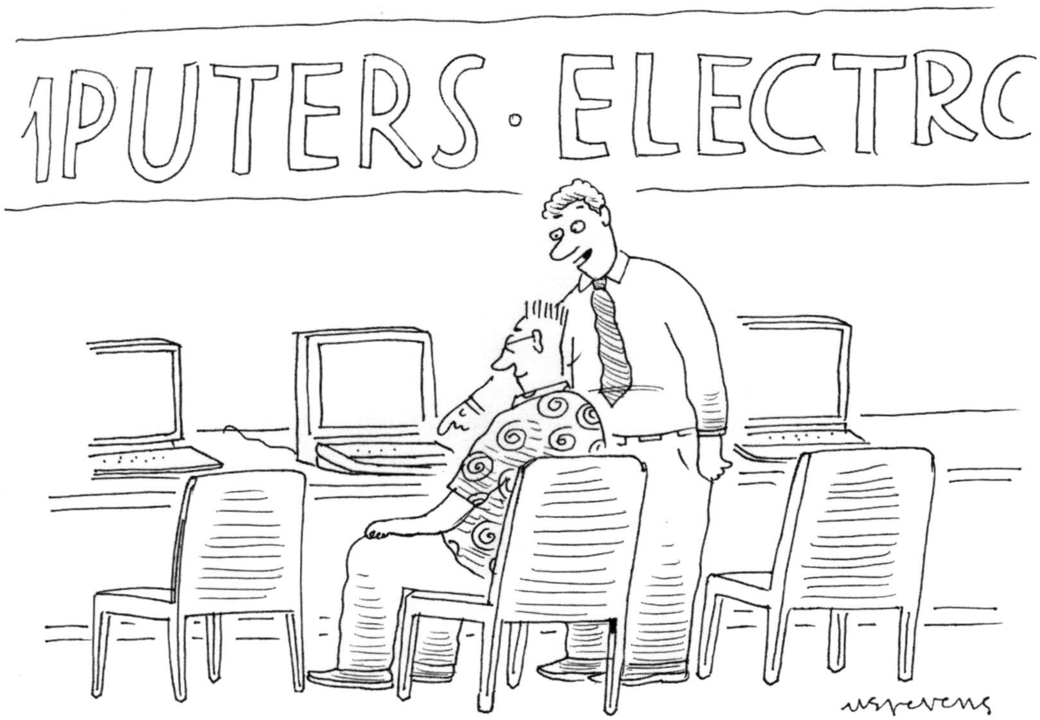

1PUTERS · ELECTRC

"Let's say you want to write an award-winning short story—you just push this key, here…"

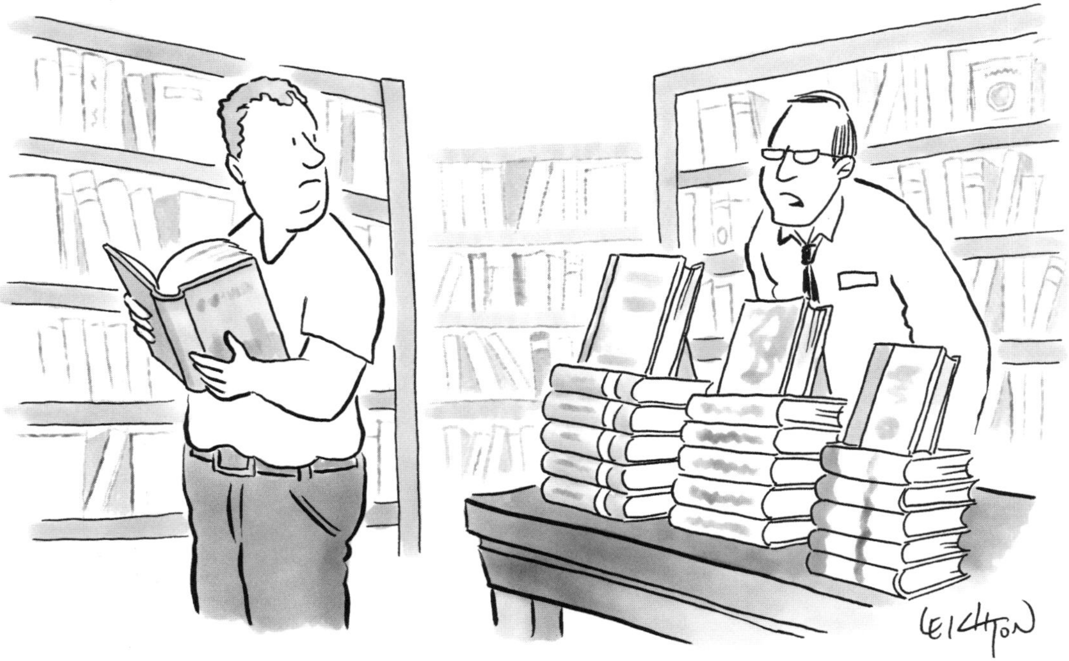
LEIGHTON

“Sir, please don’t read all the endings.”

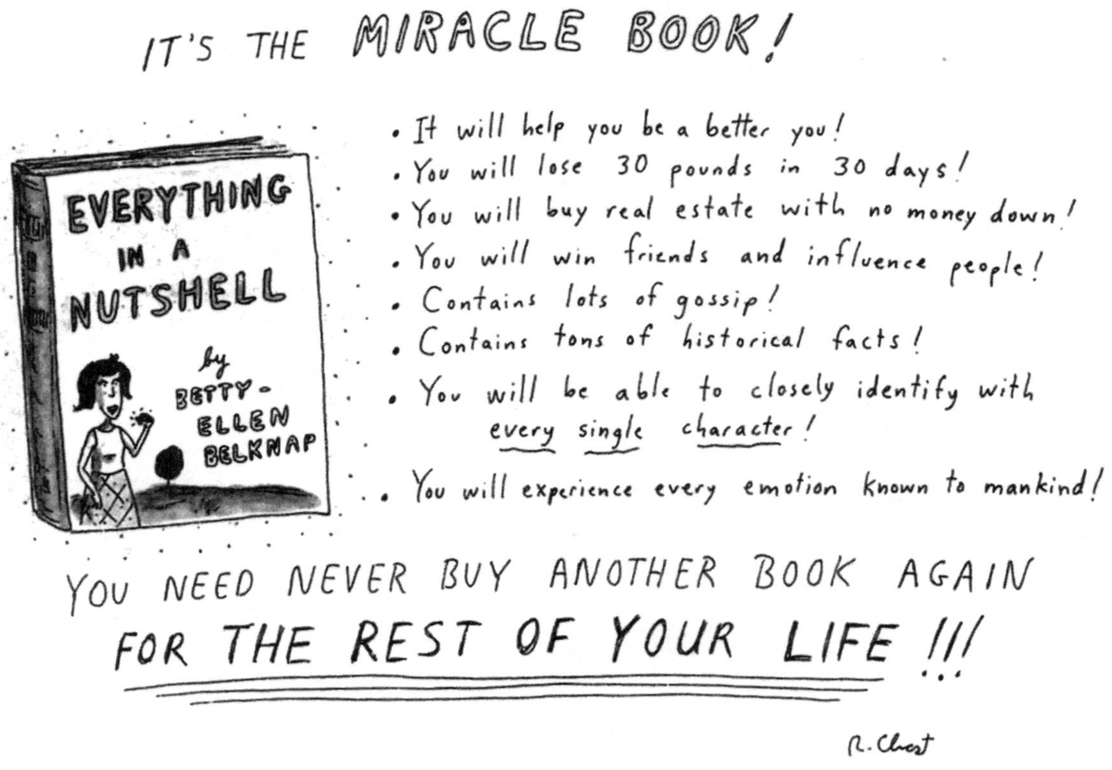
IT'S THE MIRACLE BOOK!
EVERYTHING IN A NUTSHELL
by BETTY-ELLEN BELKNAP
• It will help you be a better you!
• You will lose 30 pounds in 30 days!
• You will buy real estate with no money down!
• You will win friends and influence people!
• Contains lots of gossip!
• Contains tons of historical facts!
• You will be able to closely identify with every single character!
• You will experience every emotion known to mankind!
YOU NEED NEVER BUY ANOTHER BOOK AGAIN FOR THE REST OF YOUR LIFE!!!
R. Chast

"And for God's sake don't let anyone finish my novel!"

Contributors

Marisa Acocella (43) is the author of the *New York Times* bestselling graphic novels *Ann Tenna, Cancer Vixen*, and *Just Who the Hell is She, Anyway?* She is a *New Yorker* cartoonist whose cartoons have also appeared in *O* magazine, *Glamour*, *W*, the *New York Times*, and other publications.

George Booth (7, 111) has been a *New Yorker* cartoonist and cover artist since 1969. The National Cartoonists Society recognized his work with the Best Gag Cartoonist of the Year (1993) and the Milton Caniff Lifetime Achievement Award (2010).

David Borchart (19, 32, 82, 104) is a cartoonist for the *New Yorker*, and his cartoons have appeared in *Esquire* and *Time* magazine. His serial cartoon *A Prisoner of Ghoul Island* can be seen online at ghoulisland.com.

Pat Byrnes (38, 63) has been a cartoonist for the *New Yorker* since 1998 and is a winner of the National Cartoonists Society's Best Gag Cartoonist of the Year (2017). Previous careers include voice actor, ad copywriter, and aerospace engineer.

Roz Chast (12, 45, 61, 68, 138) is an award winning *New Yorker* cartoonist and *New York Times* bestselling author. Her new book is *Going Into Town: A Love Letter to New York*.

Frank Cotham (24, 59, 99) sold his first cartoon to the *New Yorker* in 1993. Since then he has sold over 750 cartoons to the magazine. His work can be seen at the Cartoon Bank (cartoonbank.com).

Liza Donnelly (15, 36) is an award-winning cartoonist and writer for the *New Yorker*, and is resident cartoonist at *CBS News*. Donnelly's book *Women On Men* was a finalist for the Thurber Prize for American Humor; and her history of women cartoonists, *Funny Ladies: The New Yorker's Greatest Women Cartoonists and Their Cartoons*, is considered a resource for historians.

Nick Downes (22, 73, 79, 92, 96, 106, 127) dedicated himself to becoming a magazine cartoonist back when there were magazines. He persisted in this endeavor after learning that his fallback career, pinsetter, had also become obsolete.

Bob Eckstein (20, 46, 74, 91, 95, 107, 124) is a snowman expert (see *The Illustrated History of the Snowman*) and a *New York Times* bestselling author. His work can be seen at bobeckstein. com and he can be followed at @Bob_Eckstein.

Liana Finck's (135) work appears regularly in the *New Yorker*. Her most recent graphic novel is *Passing for Human*, published by Random House in 2018.

Alex Gregory (14, 93) is a Hollywood screenwriter. His work can be seen at the Cartoon Bank (cartoonbank.com).

Sam Gross (9, 27, 31, 33, 44, 54, 72, 77, 80, 84, 90, 114, 116) has created around thirty thousand cartoons. He has published many cartoon books and was the cartoon editor for *National Lampoon*, *Smoke*, and *Parents* magazine.

William Haefeli's (23, 26, 62, 69) cartoons have been appearing in the *New Yorker* since 1998. He lives in Los Angeles.

Sid Harris (47, 67) has published thousands of cartoons. Many can be seen at sciencecartoons plus.com.

Bruce Eric Kaplan (16, 56, 64, 108, 120, 126, 131) is a cartoonist for the *New Yorker* and a television writer and producer.

Edward Koren (21, 42, 49, 52, 55, 71, 87, 101) has contributed to the *New Yorker* since 1962. He has been a Guggenheim Fellow and was Vermont's Cartoonist Laureate from 2015 to 2018.

Robert Leighton (10, 39, 70, 89, 119, 125, 137) (robert-leighton.com) has been contributing to the *New Yorker* since 2002. As a puzzle-writer, he cowrote *The New Yorker Book of Cartoon Puzzles and Games*.

Arnie Levin (75, 123) is a cartoonist, illustrator, and animation director. His work can be seen at the Cartoon Bank (cartoonbank.com), plus he is covered from head to toes in tattoos.

Bob Mankoff (41) has published over 950 cartoons in the *New Yorker*, where he was cartoon editor for twenty years. He is now the cartoon and humor editor at *Esquire* magazine.

Michael Maslin (37, 98, 117, 130) began contributing to the *New Yorker* in 1977. His website, *Ink Spill*, is devoted to *New Yorker* cartoonists and cartoons.

Paul Noth (76, 85) is a staff cartoonist for the *New Yorker*, where his work has appeared regularly since 2004. He has written for *Late Night with Conan O'Brien* and was an animation consultant for *Saturday Night Live*. He is the author of the middle-grade novels *How to Sell Your Family to the Aliens* and *How to Properly Dispose of Planet Earth*. His work can be seen at paulnoth.com.

John O'Brien's (28, 129) work can be found in many publications, including the *New Yorker*, and in over one hundred children's books. He can be found living in South Jersey or at johnobrienillustrator.com.

Danny Shanahan (30, 57) has had more than 1,200 cartoons and a dozen covers published in the *New Yorker*, as well many other publications, including *Esquire, Fortune, Playboy*, and the *New York Times*. He has published four anthologies of his work and has appeared in dozens of *New Yorker* collections. He lives in Rhinebeck, New York.

Michael Shaw (58, 112) has contributed cartoons to the *New Yorker* since 1999. Further proof of his peculiar cartooning efforts can be found at myshawrona.wixsite.com/website.

Barbara Smaller's (48, 113, 133) cartoons have appeared in numerous publications, anthologies, and, since 1996, regularly in the *New Yorker*. She is currently working on a book based on drawings from her *Course of Empire* series that has been featured in the *New Yorker's* Daily Shouts.

Edward Steed (11, 88) has been a cartoonist for the *New Yorker* since 2013.

Peter Steiner (35, 97, 100, 109) is a cartoonist, painter, and novelist. You can see some of his work at plsteiner.com.

Mick Stevens (8, 18, 65, 103, 105, 110, 122, 136, 139) has been drawing cartoons for the *New Yorker* for over thirty-five years. His books include *A Mystery, Wrapped in an Enigma, Served on a Bed of Lettuce, If Ducks Carried Guns*, and *Things Not to Do Today* and a newer e-book called *I Really Should Be Drawing: The Blook*, available online.

Julia Suits (121) is a *New Yorker* cartoonist and freelance illustrator. She lives in Austin, Texas. To see more of her projects, visit juliasuits.net.

P.C. Vey's (17, 51, 53, 78, 115, 128, 134) cartoons regularly appear in the *New Yorker*. His work also has been published in *Harvard Business Review, Barron's, National Lampoon*, the *Wall Street Journal*, the *New York Times, Prospect, Playboy, AARP Bulletin*, and the *Boston Globe*. He has had three collections of cat cartoons published by Penguin/Plume and has contributed to many books of cartoons on a variety of subjects.

Kim Warp (29, 66) began contributing to the *New Yorker* in 1999 and is a winner of the National Cartoonists Society's Best Gag Cartoonist of the Year (2000). She frequently contributes the *New Yorker's* Daily Cartoon.

Christopher Weyant (25, 40, 50, 86) is a cartoonist for the *New Yorker* and an editorial cartoonist for the *Boston Globe*. In 2015, he won the Theodor Seuss Geisel Award for his picture book *You Are (Not) Small*, written by Anna Kang. Follow him at christopherweyant.com and on Instagram @christopherweyant.

Jack Ziegler (13, 34, 60, 81, 83, 94, 102, 118, 132) was a cartoonist for the *New Yorker* from 1974 to 2017. During his lifetime he produced over 24,000 cartoons, and sold over 3,000 mainly to the *New Yorker*. You can find his work at jackziegler.com.

Published by
Princeton Architectural Press
A McEvoy Group company
202 Warren Street, Hudson, NY 12534
Visit our website at www.papress.com

Princeton Architectural Press is a leading publisher in architecture, design, photography, landscape, and visual culture. We create fine books and stationery of unsurpassed quality and production values. With more than one thousand titles published, we find design everywhere and in the most unlikely places.

Printed in China
22 21 20 19 4 3 2 1 First edition

Editor: Kristen Hewitt
Book design: Princeton Architectural Press
Front cover: Sam Gross
Back cover: Bob Eckstein

Special thanks to: Paula Baver, Janet Behning, Abby Bussel, Benjamin English, Jan Cigliano Hartman, Susan Hershberg, Stephanie Holstein, Lia Hunt, Valerie Kamen, Jennifer Lippert, Sara McKay, Parker Menzimer, Eliana Miller, Nina Pick, Wes Seeley, Rob Shaeffer, Sara Stemen, Marisa Tesoro, Paul Wagner, and Joseph Weston of Princeton Architectural Press
—Kevin C. Lippert, publisher

Thanks to Jaylen Amaker and Joy Tutela
—Bob Eckstein

For permission to reprint cartoons, on pages listed, we gratefully thank the cartoonists and the following publications:
Barron's 74, 115
Chronicle of Higher Education 91
Funny Times 95
Harvard Business Review 134
New Yorker 7, 8, 9, 10, 11, 13, 14, 16, 17, 18, 19, 23, 24, 25, 28, 29, 30, 32, 33, 34, 35, 36, 37, 40, 42, 43, 48, 49, 50, 51, 52, 54, 56, 57, 59, 60, 64, 65, 66, 68, 69, 71, 75, 76, 82, 83, 85, 86, 87, 88, 90, 93, 94, 99, 100, 101, 102, 103, 104, 105, 108, 110, 113, 116, 118, 120, 121, 126, 127, 128, 131, 132, 133, 135, 138
The Oldie 22
Prospect 107
The Spectator 73, 79
The Weekly Standard 92
Writer's Digest 46

Library of Congress Cataloging-in-Publication Data:
Names: Eckstein, Bob, editor.
Title: The ultimate cartoon book of book cartoons by the world's greatest cartoonists / Bob Eckstein, editor.
Description: First edition. | New York : Princeton Architectural Press, [2019]
Identifiers: LCCN 2018043289 | ISBN 9781616898045 (hardcover : alk. paper)
Subjects: LCSH: American wit and humor, Pictorial. | Caricatures and cartoons—United States.
Classification: LCC NC1426 .U48 2019 | DDC 741.5/6973—dc23
LC record available at https://lccn.loc.gov/2018043289